Raising Girls

Raising Girls

How to Help Your Daughter Grow Up
Happy, Healthy, and Strong

Steve Biddulph

TEN SPEED PRESS
Berkeley

Originally published worldwide (except in the United States)
by HarperCollins in 2013.

Photographs courtesy of the author with the following exceptions:
page 54 © Monkey Business Images/Shutterstock; page 80 © Louise Mitchell;
page 82 © Harriet Atkins; page 92 © Brook Curran; page 95 © Barry Durdant-
Hollamby; page 115 © Alexey Lysenko/Shutterstock; page 120 © Serg Shalimoff/
Shutterstock; page 174 © Michael Jung/Shutterstock; page 196 © Louise Mitchell

Library of Congress Cataloging-in-Publication Data
Biddulph, Steve.
  Raising girls : how to help your daughter grow up happy, healthy, and strong /
Steve Biddulph. — First US Edition.
      pages cm
  Includes bibliographical references and index.
  1. Girls. 2. Parenting. 3. Child rearing. I. Title.
  HQ777.B53 2014
  305.23082--dc23
                          2013047076

Trade Paperback ISBN: 978-1-60774-575-4
eISBN: 978-1-60774-576-1

Printed in the United States of America

Design by Colleen Cain

10 9 8 7 6 5 4 3 2 1

First US Edition

Contents

A Letter from Steve

Dear Reader,

It's amazing what you learn about yourself. Twenty years ago, when we were expecting our second child, friends naturally asked what we were hoping for, a boy or a girl? I always said I didn't mind, and I really believed that was true. We already had a boy of seven, and we were very eager simply to have another child.

We had planned on having a homebirth, but it ended as an emergency caesarian—that's what we do every time in our family! So I found myself standing in the operating room, trying my best not to faint. Then from Shaaron's belly the medical team pulled a slippery bundle, and somebody said, "Well done, you've got a little girl!" Suddenly I was crying. And laughing. And jumping around. I was, in short, incredibly happy. I hadn't realized how much I wanted a daughter. I was holding her and looking at her for hours afterward, just amazed. That was all those years ago, and the feeling hasn't gone away.

Daughters evoke such strong feelings in us—protectiveness, awe, hope, and fear, but mostly just a fierce love and a wish to give them the best possible life.

*   *   *

For more than twenty years, I had a specialty in boys and men. It wasn't a choice so much as a mission—back then, boys were a disaster zone, and urgently in need of help. I wrote the world's top-selling book on raising boys, with a simple message that they needed to be strongly loved and firmly taught how to be good men, that they needed positive role models, and that their energy wasn't a bad thing.

Back then, girls were doing fine. Then, in the mid-2000s, that started to change. We began to see a sudden and marked plunge in girls' mental health, first in the United States but quickly spreading across the world. Problems such as eating disorders and self-harm, which had once been extremely rare, were now happening in every school and on almost every street. But more than this, the average girl, everygirl, was stressed and depressed in a way we hadn't seen before.

Girls aren't born hating their own bodies. They aren't born angry at life. Something was happening in the culture that was poisoning girls' spirits. It seemed to come on as they entered their teens, but it was creeping up on them younger and younger.

In response, a worldwide movement sprang up—of girl advocates, therapists, and researchers—to try to mobilize parents and the community. Many of these people were my friends, and together we saw the need for a simple parent-friendly book to help get girlhood back on track.

Raising strong girls starts far, far back, when they are tiny or toddlers, or just in elementary school. We have to love them well, and we have to fight the big world, too, since the predators that want to bring our daughters down are everywhere; they wear suits and make good money and have no conscience at all. The choices we make in the way we raise our daughters can help keep their spirits alive and their self-belief strong, even when the world sends a very different message.

Girlhood is a quest, a journey of gathering the wisdom needed to be a woman. We are our daughters' guides on that quest. We need good maps, good stories, and clear eyes.

What could be more awesome than to see your daughter standing tall, wise, and strong at twenty-five or forty, and knowing that you helped to make her so? And what could be more worthwhile than to fight for a world that is open for all young girls, wherever they are born, to be able to realize their dreams?

I hope this book thrills you and helps you pass on to your daughter all the love you feel.

Warmly,
Steve Biddulph

Meet Kaycee and Genevieve

There are two girls that I would like you to meet. Their names are Kaycee and Genevieve. Both are seventeen, and both are seniors in high school. They are great kids, friendly and bright; you would enjoy talking to them.

These two have known each other since preschool. They were best friends all through elementary school and everyone thought they would be that way forever. But around the time Kaycee and Genevieve moved up to high school, something went wrong between them. The reason is hard to say—I am not sure they could even pin it down themselves; but today, if they pass in the school corridor, they feel that awkwardness that comes from having once been friends.

Kaycee and Genevieve's lives have taken very different paths. I'm going to tell you their stories, because they make really clear the dangers, and the hopes, of girlhood today.

Kaycee's Story

Let's meet Kaycee first. On first impression, Kaycee seems a very grown-up seventeen-year-old. She wears carefully applied makeup and ultrafashionable clothes, and she speaks fast and in a clear voice. This much confidence in a teenager may be quite genuine, but if you know young people well, you might wonder if Kaycee has possibly become "too old too soon." And there is something else that you might notice. It's in her manner. Her expression is world-weary. When she speaks, she sounds rather cynical and hard. For a seventeen-year-old, *she doesn't seem to be having a lot of fun.*

Back when Kaycee was fourteen, something big did happen. It wasn't the stuff of newspaper headlines, but it was a significant experience that affected the direction of her life.

Halfway through freshman year, Kaycee was invited to a classmate's birthday party. The parents hosting the party had implied a somewhat higher level of supervision than they actually provided on the night. So the party went pretty much as it would if forty or fifty kids of varying ages were left in a house at night with lots of alcohol and no adults in sight: loud, chaotic, and out of control. Kaycee found it very exciting—in particular because a boy she knew, Ciaran, who was seventeen and two years above her in school, was there. Kaycee and her friends had often admired Ciaran at school, with his good looks and cool demeanor, but tonight there was something different—he was noticing *her*. Then, amazingly, it got better still. He sat with her, and they talked and had a few drinks. They talked and snuggled a little in the garden. She could hardly believe her luck (it was all she could manage not to take out her phone and text someone!). After a while, Ciaran stood up, took her by the hand, and led her upstairs to one of the many bedrooms in this big, fancy house apparently devoid of adults. They had sex.

It all went faster than Kaycee had imagined her first sexual experience would, and it was less tender, too. Blurred by the alcohol, Kaycee's brain wasn't really working very well; she was aware, though, of the shift from the excited feeling of being special and the center of Ciaran's attention, to physical discomfort and a sense of being pushed about, invaded, not really noticed as a person. When it was over, which was quite soon, Ciaran managed a kiss before straightening his clothes and leaving the room. When Kaycee got herself together and went out into the party, she felt unsure and shaky. Then she saw Ciaran, standing with a group of friends, who all looked at her and smirked. She realized in an instant that he had been telling them of his "conquest." Tears burned her face, she fled from the house and ended up in the garden, sobbing. A friend tried to comfort her, but Kaycee wouldn't say what had happened.

She went home that night in a kind of icy rage. She hated Ciaran now, and for a while boys in general. Kaycee was a spirited girl, she had been independent all her life, her busy parents valued self-sufficiency. She told no one what had happened. (When her parents finally learned about it three years later in a family counseling session, they were saddened and shocked.) But like millions of girls before her who had first sexual experiences they regretted or did not enjoy, Kaycee hid her wounds and got on with her life. But she was a changed girl.

Did the experience put her off boys? Not at all. What it put her off was *vulnerability*, being the one who was used. She began sleeping with boys on her own initiative, and on her own terms. She chose them, and she called the shots. By the age of seventeen, when she first spoke to a counselor, Kaycee had had sex with seven different boys. Possibly eight, there was a night where some alcohol-affected confusion had occurred, and she wasn't sure.

Now, three years later, Kaycee has stabilized somewhat, she has a steady boyfriend. But she doesn't hold him in very high regard and confides that she is "planning to ditch him sometime soon."

We know from research (and from most people's recollections of their own teenage years), that Kaycee's experience is not uncommon. Perhaps, one could argue, we just need to be less uptight about teen sex and let them make their own mistakes, and learn from them. (That is also a convenient argument for those parents who prefer not to get involved, or are too busy to keep a close eye on their kids.) But let's stay with the story . . .

Kaycee's life, at this point in time, isn't going very well. Her parents didn't seek help because of her sex life, which they were only vaguely aware of, and in a sense didn't want to know about. Their concern was that her drinking was getting out of control (she was not yet, of course, of drinking age), and she was failing at her expensive private school. She was halfway through senior year, and the school was concerned about her poor grades and her many absences from class. The family had been advised to "see someone" about her problems. When she arrived with her parents to meet with a counselor, Kaycee looked angry to have been brought there. But within half an hour, and given a sympathetic listener, she was pouring out her feelings.

The family's seeking help—not just for Kaycee, but for themselves—was a brave step, and in fact proved to be a turning point. We will return to Kaycee and her parents at the very end of the book, to let you know how it all worked out.

A Marked and Sudden Change

In the last ten years, there has been a big change in the lives of girls. And it's affecting them at every age, from babyhood to teens. While the same wishes and dreams are there for girls journeying toward womanhood that we had in our day, the world is forcing changes on them that are on a whole different scale. In particular, things are beginning to happen when they are younger.

This is a key point to keep in mind about girls' situation today, and it was first made by psychologist Mary Pipher in her ground breaking book *Reviving Ophelia*. To understand our daughters, we have to realize that their childhood is not like ours. To put it bluntly, our eighteen is their fourteen. Our fourteen is their ten. That's in terms of the pressures, the behaviors, and what they are supposed to be and act like according to the peer norms that exist today—and our failure to protect them, for we are partly responsible. We—and that's all of us, parents, relatives, friends, and society—are not supporting girlhood in the way we once did. We haven't put enough adult time and care around our daughters, or taught them well enough.

In the last ten years, a greedy corporate world has realized that girls, and especially *preteen* girls, are a soft target. Companies saw that there were enormous profits to be made in exploiting their anxieties (or in fact creating those anxieties) about everything from skin to weight to friendship to clothes to even making it into adulthood. In boardrooms and advertising agencies, magazines and media outlets, the war on girls began. And it succeeded. Everywhere she looks, today's young girl sees messages that make her feel she is not good enough, that imprison her in cramped and narrow ideas of how she is supposed to look, think, and act. Never before has girlhood been under such a sustained assault, ranging through everything from diet ads, alcohol marketing, fashion pressures, to the inroads of hard pornography into teenage bedrooms.

The result is that many girls have lost four *years* of childhood peace, development, and stability. They are being forced out of childhood when they have not yet completed it, or even fully enjoyed it. The result is girls in enormous pain and confusion. They try to act grown up, but they can't. They are filling up mental health clinics, police stations, emergency rooms, and alcohol and drug treatment programs in numbers never seen before.

If we are awake to what is going on, we can improve this situation— through the love we give, the environment we create for them with supports and interests, and through the protection we offer from the stupid and exploitive media messages from the world around them. I have a favorite saying that has often helped me: "We can't stop the birds of sorrow from flying through our lives, but we don't have to let them make nests in our hair!" We can live in this world, but we don't have to swallow everything it offers us. We can choose for ourselves and for our daughters the experiences that make us strong, happy, and alive. That's what Genevieve and her parents did . . .

Genevieve's Story

Genevieve, like Kaycee, is also seventeen, also in her senior year. On first meeting, Genevieve seems a little nervous and shy, but she soon relaxes when she gets to know you. Her conversation is full of ideas, concerns, funny stories, and perspectives on things. She switches in a moment from excited child to thoughtful young adult, as is typical of someone just on the edge of womanhood. She doesn't have the tough exterior of Kaycee, but then, perhaps she doesn't need to. Her story is a very different one.

Genevieve does not have a boyfriend right now. She would love to, but is wary; she knows that young love is not always easy. Also, she finds the boys of her own age frustratingly hard to hold a conversation with and longs to meet more mature, communicative boys when she goes to college.

Genevieve's friends at school are a warm and friendly bunch, not the high flyers, but the quieter, more natural kids. They look out for each other and also, if there is a newcomer or someone left on the outer edges of the group, they are more likely to include them and make them welcome. As a result, they are a large, ramshackle group, slightly dorky and uncool, but not too worried about it.

Genevieve did go out with a boy at fifteen, and this was an intense experience for her. Justin was her own age, and they met early in the school year. They spent time together as often as they could, taking long walks, holding hands, having soulful conversations. He was more experienced sexually, though, and after a few months, he began pressuring Genevieve to "go further" when they were alone together. Other girls had had sex with him in the past, and he really wanted this with Genevieve, too.

Genevieve is close to her mother and accustomed to talking over pretty much everything in her life with her. In fact, her mother joked that for every hour spent with Justin, Genevieve spent another hour discussing what had taken place, what he said, what it might mean, what she said back, and so on! While many girls do this detailed debriefing with their friends, Genevieve was used to discussing her innermost thoughts with her mom, and so this new problem naturally became part of their ongoing conversation. As a result, her mom was involved in dealing with this new sexual pressure on her daughter and able to offer her help.

To her great credit, Genevieve's mom did not panic and did not try to take control of the situation by telling Genevieve what to do. She later told me that she would have, if necessary, brought in some limits on how and where the pair could meet, since they were below the legal age, as well as the wise age, to start having sex. In other words, she would not allow her daughter, at just fifteen, to be out of her depth in a situation where she might not be emotionally and physically safe. At the same time, Genevieve's mom supported, cautiously, her wish to have a friendship with a boy. She would drive her daughter into town to meet Justin to go to a movie or meet up with friends, or bring him over to visit their house.

This remarkably sensible mother had a low-key but thoughtful response to her daughter's questions. Instead of "laying down the law" as a first strategy, she simply helped Genevieve to explore her own wants. *What did she feel she wanted? What was her body telling her? What did she think was the course of action she would feel good about, long term?*

She did this in a quiet, casual kind of way that gave Genevieve real space to reflect. Her mom had that knack of listening intently without pressure, so that Genevieve knew that she had her full attention, and so her thoughts and feelings tumbled out effortlessly.

Genevieve's inner signals were quite clear. She really liked Justin, she liked being with him, but she felt uneasy and rather crowded when he was too physical with her. It was all a bit too intense. She hoped their relationship would strengthen and grow, but she wanted it to take its time. Her mother listened, and nodded, and reflected back to her daughter, "It sounds like you really aren't ready to have sex with him. You don't want it to go that way right away?" Genevieve said no, but she was worried what would happen if she rejected Justin's advances repeatedly. They talked over how she could let Justin know her feelings and wants.

Over the next few weeks, Genevieve and Justin did have a kind of debate about this. He basically gave his own ultimatum, in response to hers, and there was a real testing of wills. Justin knew plenty of girls who, though not quite as interesting or special as Genevieve, were willing to offer him sex, and in the end, he "walked." She had known this was a real possibility, but that did not prevent her from feeling crushed. She was an open-hearted girl, almost totally without hardness or shell, and she took a long time to heal. But she did heal, and six months later, when Justin phoned to try to get back together, she was kind but clear in her refusal. She had moved on.

A Reality Check

When I was young, I loved to travel and live in remote places—from tiny villages in Papua, New Guinea, to the slums of Calcutta in West Bengal. When I returned home, I was always struck by this remarkable thing: People living in tough places were happier. Life in those places was hard, but the locals still managed to laugh and be warm to each other. (When I came back to affluence, everyone seemed miserable.) The experience convinced me that we are supposed to be *happy*. We are not meant to be depressed. Especially not at fifteen years of age.

Girlhood is supposed to be fun, with friends young and old, adventures in young love, mastery of new skills and abilities. Its dramas should be dramas of learning and growing, not of being battered and damaged.

Compared to how girlhood should be, it's clear something has gone badly wrong. Millions of parents are asking, Why are our daughters so stressed? What should we do, so that their lives turn out well? As you will soon see, there is plenty that we *can* do.

PART ONE

The Five Stages of Girlhood

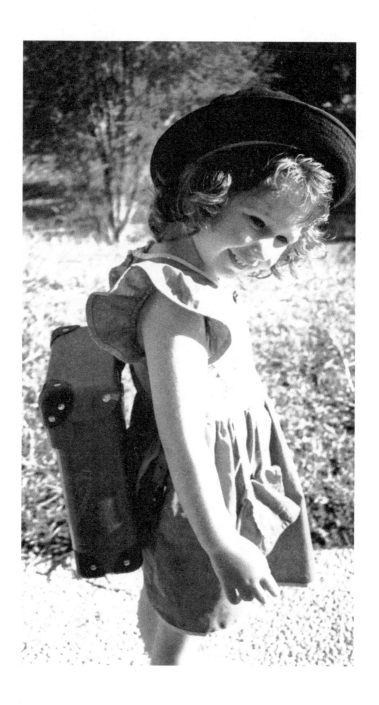

CHAPTER ONE

Creating a Total Girl

Two-year-old Mollie lifts a Tonka truck high in the air and is about to smack it down on her friend Jemima's head. Even at two, she knows this is not really in the True Spirit of Playgroup, so she glances toward where her mother is watching to see how it might go down. Her mom has seen it all and is urgently flashing her a "don't you dare" frown. Ever . . . so . . . slowly, Mollie lowers the truck to the carpet and goes back to coloring. Jemima remains blissfully unaware that anything has happened and goes on humming to herself while holding firmly onto the only yellow crayon.

Ten-year-old Elise looks at her computer screen and sees the message trashing one of the girls in her class, a girl who is already shy and insecure. It's mean and personal, and one of her own friends just posted it. Elise chews her top lip so hard it leaves a red mark. She hates bullying, but how can she intervene and not make enemies? She heads downstairs to talk to her mom.

Fifteen-year-old Samantha pauses during the math exam, draws a deep breath, and frowns. She has almost finished, with loads of time to spare. If she keeps going, she will probably top the class; she likes math and always does well, but then she will be seen as a "brain," which is highly uncool, especially with boys. She knows she can just stop now and leave out the last couple of questions. *Nah!* she exclaims to herself, then worries if she said that out loud. Nobody seems to have noticed. She gets on and finishes the exam.

Girlhood is a lot of fun, for parents and for girls themselves, but it also has its intense times. At each stage of their growing up, girls have to deal with difficult decisions. They get confused and make mistakes, but eventually they learn and grow, and out of all this they become capable and strong adult women.

As a parent, it helps to have a map of the country of childhood so that you know what to expect and what to do. The map in this book is drawn from the latest findings in child development and neuroscience, family therapy and parenting education, but it also comes from talking to mothers, fathers, and teachers in many countries. I never quite trust experts, unless what they say matches my own heart and passes the test of common sense. That comes from talking to lots of people. Eventually, the map becomes clearer. You feel like you know where you are.

The Five Stages of Girlhood

While each girl is unique, there is still a journey that all girls have to make to grow up well. Girls seem to be different from boys in the stages they go through, and the ages at which they happen. In the chapters to come, you can look up the age of your daughter and dive into more detail about what is happening for her. But first it's good to get the big picture and see where you are.

STAGE 1: SECURITY (BIRTH TO TWO YEARS)

Am I safe and loved? Human babies are the most dependent babies on earth. Born totally defenseless, babies instinctively know that the adults around them *have* to love them, or they may not give them proper care. It's not enough just to be fed and clothed. Machines could keep a baby alive, but she would not develop intelligence or kindness; she would be a very strange being indeed. It's through her parents comforting her tenderly, singing and talking to her, jiggling and tickling and loving her, that a baby girl comes fully alive, and decides that life is good. In this situation, her emotional as well as her physical needs are responded to. Out of all this, she makes a fundamental decision about life: *I am loved and safe.* And she carries that inside her, always.

Girls Do It Differently–and More Quickly

Girls develop more quickly than boys, especially in brain abilities. The estrogen their body creates while still in the womb actually increases the rate of brain growth, and at birth they are many weeks ahead of boys.

The difference increases in the first five or six years. Girls learn to speak whole sentences and control their fingers, to do neat drawings or even writing six to twelve months sooner than boys. Girls are ready to start school about a year earlier than boys. Girls do not suffer as much separation anxiety as boys if they have to go to child care—although this varies a lot with the individual child.

Girls enter puberty about two years sooner than boys do, turning into young women overnight when the boys seem to be standing still. And finally, they become adult sooner—girls' brain development finishes several years before boys finally get there in their early twenties! It's as if nature says to girls: you'd better grow up ahead of the game, you will need your wits about you!

STAGE 2: EXPLORING (TWO TO FIVE YEARS)

Is the world a fun and interesting place? This stage is when a girl learns to be confident and interested in the world around her, to be smart and creative. It builds on the secure feelings from stage 1; if people are going to stay close and care for me, I can relax and check out the toys, play in the garden, toddle out across the grass, mess about with dirt and stones and leaves.

Babies who don't feel securely attached to their parents do not explore very much; they are too afraid their mom or dad will desert them.

This is the age when your daughter can be shown how to paint, poke, build, create, and enjoy the world of things, animals, and people. If the people who love her share some of these activities with her, she will pick up on their enthusiasm and pleasure in making and doing. Her brain becomes *permanently* switched on to learning. You will have taught her that life is an adventure. Strange, new, and challenging things will be a joy for her for the rest of her life.

STAGE 3: PEOPLE SKILLS (FIVE TO TEN YEARS)

Can I get along with others? Other children, other adults, as well as Mom and Dad, brothers and sisters, can be difficult but are mostly fun. Your daughter finds that she can have better fun by sharing a little, giving way a little, cooperating and playing together, than if she is just on her own. This isn't possible until about three or four years of age, and even then it's hard. But by learning first from Mom or Dad, and then other people, she can work out that she is not the center of the universe. Other people have feelings, too.

Right through elementary school, this most complex of skills—valuing yourself, but also valuing others and treating them with respect—is gradually being learned. Again, it builds on the earlier stages: being treated kindly, you grow kind; being treated sensitively, you grow empathy; being treated honestly, you grow honest.

She decides that mostly people are fine. I like them. Let's play! Your daughter will be a "people person." For the rest of her life, she will know how to be with people in a happy and helpful way.

STAGE 4: FINDING HER SOUL (TEN TO FOURTEEN YEARS)

Can I discover my deep-down self and what makes me truly happy? With the coming of puberty, a girl starts to experience a much stronger sense of being her own person, a separate and private self. She is far from being a woman, but she is no longer a child either. Like a tree in winter, she is building up reserves for when she will be ready to blossom. These are the years in which she begins to strengthen the "inside" of her deep self—who she really is. It's a time when she needs help to think about what she stands for and cares most deeply about, and also what her interests and passions are. Often at this age a girl finds her "spark"—something she loves to do that gives her joy, purpose, and a creative way to make a contribution—a reason to be alive.

By gaining an identity through doing and believing and strengthening her inner world, a girl will be freer from the need for approval that haunts many teen girls and makes them conformist and dull.

A girl's soul is like a wild animal, powerful and savvy but wary, too. It needs time and quiet to emerge. As a girl finds her soul, she will be equipped to face the big questions of life: choosing intimacy on her own terms, choosing her career path, knowing which peer group to hang around with. A girl who knows her own soul may be a gentle girl, but also one who has a steel in her, not easily manipulated by careless boys or false friends. She will be loyal, tough, and protective of those around her. And of herself.

STAGE 5: STEPPING INTO ADULTHOOD (FOURTEEN TO EIGHTEEN YEARS)

Can I take responsibility for my own life? At eighteen, your daughter begins to be a woman; so at the age of fourteen, the preparation for that huge leap has to begin in earnest. It's mostly practical—here's how you manage money, time, eating, clothes, health, safety, driving a car—but it's also time for a powerful shift in attitude. Sometime between fourteen and adulthood, a girl needs some kind of marker event, a growing-up rite, an experience or even misfortune that teaches her that she is now at the steering wheel of her *own* life,

Think of Your Own Life

If you are a mother, you have a huge advantage in raising a daughter—you used to be one. If you are a dad, it's different, but daughters don't expect their dads to be their moms, usually, so it's all right. You have a different part to play that is just as important.

If you're a mom reading this, think back to your own childhood. (It's still worth doing this if you're a dad, though the stages would have been somewhat different.)

* Did you feel safe and secure when you were a baby? Were your parents in a good place in their lives and able to really love and enjoy you?

* Were you encouraged to play, enjoy, and explore the world around you? Did your parents have the time and interest to excite you and show you how good life was as a toddler?

* When you went to school, did your parents help you and show you how to get along with others? Could they get along with others themselves? Could they look out for themselves but also respect the needs of others?

* Did you find in your early teens that your unique interests were supported, or were people too busy?

* Did you find in your midteens that you could get to know your own soul and connection to nature and the universe, and be strengthened in this?

* And finally, in your late teens, did you have a clear transition to being adult, where you felt that you took control of your own life, faced the consequences of your actions, and had a sense of power as well as a purpose?

Lots of questions, but you will quickly work out where you did okay and where things fell down. Perhaps that will help you know how to get it right for your daughter, and how important that is.

that she literally holds her life in her own hands. This is a frightening realization, but frightening in a good way. By steadying herself, and by receiving the welcome and support of older women, she can leave behind childishness or harmful gullibility and be accountable, connected to consequences and proactive in making her life worthwhile. While life itself can deliver this realization to a girl, leaving it to chance is a hazardous and unreliable way for it to happen. She might come to serious harm. Also, some people never grow up and their lives are self-absorbed and wasted; they drift in misery, blame everyone else, and never take responsibility.

Girls have to be deliberately and proactively launched into healthy womanhood. When this is done well, the results are impressive. A girl takes charge of her life and makes her unique way in the world.

Each Stage Asks a Question

I hope you'll find the five stages clear and easy to understand. Remember that each girl is different, so the stages can vary quite a lot according to the age at which they happen. Also, they overlap, because nature is efficient and starts one lesson while the other is still finishing. I hope you can live with that!

The key point is that *as your daughter completes each stage, she comes to a decision about her life*, which is going to either help or harm her. For example, imagine a girlhood where all five stages go badly. This girl would arrive at the following five decisions:

1. Life is uncertain, and nobody loves me.

2. New ideas and things are frightening.

3. People can't be trusted, and they are impossible to get along with.

4. I have nothing of value inside me. I am a nobody.

5. Growing up is just too hard. I don't want to be an adult. I don't have any power or any choice in what happens to me. Stuff just happens.

Those are pretty bad outcomes, but they are familiar to anyone who works with girls. Every parent can look at their daughter, and her friends, and other girls in their town and city and see the results of these stages being lived out. Some girls will make it, some will not. The decisions that girls make at each stage are profound and life altering.

Fortunately (in case you are now paralyzed with fear!), these decisions are made little by little, combining many experiences, so we shouldn't panic about always getting things right. The stages last for years, and we get lots of chances.

As a parent, what matters is that you don't give up. Loving your daughter and always trying are what will get you through. And if your daughter is already past some of the stages and you feel that she didn't really get the message, don't despair, those decisions can often be remade later.

Of course, if you have a new little baby daughter, and she is the reason you are reading this book, then you are lucky indeed. But at any age, if you have enough caring and motivation, then you can still put things right.

Using the Stages

Use the stages by asking, what age is your girl? What is the most likely big question that her life is asking, according to the stages listed above? (Always check with your own experience, rather than letting books or theories dictate your actions.) If your gut feeling is that this *is* the stage she is in, you can organize the experiences and inputs to help her along. I will teach you how in the chapters to come.

Another use of the stages is remedial; you can pinpoint the earlier stages that she might have missed out on, due to difficult circumstances. The nature of human beings is that we can often recover things that we missed out on by getting them down the track. For example, adopted children from terrible backgrounds can gradually find security with their new parents. Overprotected girls

Clingy for a Reason

Gemma, age ten, is very clingy and always needs cuddles and closeness from her mom.

At first, her mom finds this annoying, but then she remembers something—that she was very stressed and suffered depression when Gemma was a baby. She realizes that Gemma, though really in stage 3, is going back to complete her stage 1 "Am I loved and safe?" She decides to really give Gemma all the hugs that she seems to need and finds that it makes a huge difference. Her daughter relaxes more and becomes much more confident and independent within a couple of months.

Under Stress, We All Regress!

Here's a handy tip. Sometimes when a family is under stress, kids will deal with this by dropping back a stage. A confident five-year-old will suddenly suck her thumb and want to wrap herself up in a blanket. A fourteen-year-old would rather hang out with you at a party or barbecue than mix with the other kids. Or a twenty-one-year-old will refuse to make a decision for herself and want to be told what to do.

Under stress, we all drop back a stage or two—think of those times when you just don't want to get out of bed, or just don't want to deal with people. That's quite normal from time to time. Generally, let your daughter regenerate and recuperate in this way—nobody can handle reality all of the time. You only need to worry if she doesn't seem to "grow up" after a few days. She might need nudging out of it or some more help to find out what is wrong.

Be sure you find out the reason why she is stressed, if there is no obvious explanation. There may be something she needs to tell you that she is finding hard to talk about.

Be gentle on yourself, too, so she can see that everyone needs nurture and to slow down. Lowering your whole family's stress levels with vacations, having one day of the week as a rest day, and less overscheduling generally means that she won't be as likely to go into overload. Often a stressed child is an indicator that the whole family needs to slow down.

who are fearful can be challenged and coaxed to show more courage. Girls with no people skills can learn to get along better, and so on. Be open to the possibility that your daughter may be a certain age in years but a far younger age in development, if she missed out due to life circumstance during the earlier parts of her "quest."

In a Nutshell

* All girls go through five stages to become a woman.

* These stages teach her the five big lessons of growing up: being secure, learning to explore, relating to other people, finding her soul, and taking charge of her life. Adult help is needed for all of these, and the adults have to know what to do.

* Parents who know the map of girlhood can organize their lives to provide what is needed.

* It's your daughter who makes the journey, but you are her coaches, caregivers, and allies along the way. Taking on these roles is probably the best thing you will ever do.

CHAPTER TWO

Right from the Start (Birth to Two Years)

It's early morning and little Lucy, just five weeks old, is lying wide awake in her crib beside her parents' bed. Her mom and dad are both asleep; in fact, her dad is lightly snoring. Lucy watches the dancing shadows made by the sunlight on the wall. From time to time, she waves her arms in sheer delight. She makes happy noises, and her head turns from side to side as she takes in the wonder of the world.

After a while, Lucy starts to feel hungry. She whimpers, and her mother, ears attuned for her baby's sounds by a million years of mammalian history, wakes up, even though her husband's snoring has not disturbed her all night. She reaches over and sleepily brings Lucy into the bed, then uncovers a milk-swollen breast for her to suckle on. Lucy hasn't needed to get upset, so she settles happily to feed, fully alert, looking into her mom's eyes as she does so. At this age, the focal length of her eyes is fixed at just the right distance to her mother's face when feeding, about twelve inches, anything farther away is still blurred. All she needs to see clearly is that her mom is happy and content. Then she can relax, too.

Soon the day will begin. Lucy and her mom or dad will move through different activities, going shopping, perhaps meeting or dropping in on friends. There will be many changes of diapers, many feedings. But most of this time Lucy will be just lying about, or sleeping. Eating and sleeping, without any special effort, are the main events of early babyhood. And through all of this, Lucy's brain will be growing. In just this first year of life, it will double or even triple in size. It will never grow so fast or so well as in these early months, though. It is the love, smiles, songs, and playful interactions, and all the other myriad natural things that parents do with babies, that help it to grow.

Learning to Connect

As her mom goes about her activities around the house or at her computer, if Lucy gets lonely she will make sounds to attract her mom's attention. And her mom will answer her. While Lucy will not have words for a year or so, she and her mother know exactly what the other is communicating. Roughly translated, the conversation goes like this:

> Baby: "Are you there, beloved one?"
>
> Mom: "Yes, I am!"
>
> Baby: "Am I still the most important thing in your life?"
>
> Mom: "Yes, you are."
>
> Baby: "Just checking!"
>
> Mom: "That's fine."

Researchers have filmed these mother-baby exchanges using special high-speed cameras and have given them a scientific name: *joint attention sequences*. These are the little rituals when mother and baby check in with each other, and they happen dozens of times a day. These mini "conversations" help make this child not just secure in her mother's love, but as she gets older, better able to relate empathically and sensitively to other people. The timing is incredibly sensitive, they seem to sway and move in total harmony. Researchers found that if the mom is on a video screen, it still works;

but if they introduce a mere one-second delay, the baby completely panics. The rhythm of *this baby* and *this mother* are totally attuned. The delicate dance of interaction, with sounds and nods, smiles and bits of sing-song, shape this little girl's abilities to relate well for life. Often Lucy's cries will be more intense, if something has scared her or she has a moment of painful hunger, or because something is not to her liking. Her mother will match this startle response with, "Oooh, what's wrong?" or "Oh dear, what's the matter?" using the higher-pitched voice that adults tend to adopt around babies. This voice is more audible to a baby's ears (though nobody knew that until recently when audiologists learned how to measure it). The mother will then shift her pitch and tone to a more soothing level. She will probably pick Lucy up and rock her gently to restore some rhythmic peace. From thousands of such soothings, Lucy's brain will learn the pathway from stress to relaxation, a pathway she can use for all her life to come.

Lucy and her parents' time together will have a quality that is called *responsiveness*. Put simply, they will be tuned in to her and will get to know her ways. They will read her signals and respond, not in a panicky way, but smoothly and contentedly. Partly this is simply how love (and the hormone of love, known as oxytocin) works, but partly it's because they have made it a priority to be not too busy or rushed in these early months. (They didn't decide to renovate the bathroom or take a big promotion right now, knowing that babyhood was a pretty demanding event on its own.) Unless Lucy's mom is numbed out by drug addiction, or is suffering from depression, she will most likely find Lucy delightful to be around, though certainly demanding. Parenthood may not come naturally, but it will grow and settle into a new and satisfying rhythm, if she gives it time and if she has support from those around her.

Support from grandmas, friends, and aunties is very important. New moms or dads can't easily do this stage on their own, they need a bit of mothering, too. Love is like a river, and it has to flow in and out of us. Being close to family and friends really helps when you have a little baby.

People Skills Start Very Young

As adults, we know that people skills make a huge difference in life. We notice it most when they are not there—a hugely insensitive boss or colleague, a person in the street or in a shop who is clueless and uncaring. Awareness of other peoples' feelings, the timing of conversation, knowing when to listen and when to speak are complex and advanced skills. Most of us have had moments with another person when we were awkward, when perhaps the timing was jumbled up. Hopefully, this was just momentary; often it has happened when we were trying too hard or wanting to impress. We lost our own "realness." Some people we meet are extraordinarily engaged and sensitive, and we feel great to be with them, noticed and valued. For a social animal like us, harmonious interaction is central to our happiness.

That's why we start learning long before we can even speak. Interestingly, it's the *second* six months of human life that seem to matter the most. This is the time when a baby gets much fussier about who is around them. Mothers have known for thousands of years that a newborn can be shared around, but a six-month-old baby knows exactly who its mom and dad are, and often won't trust anyone else.

Neuroscience bears this out. It's in the second six months of life that the baby grows those areas of the brain that are specifically for

people skills. Girl babies have more aptitude and awareness of social connection, which is a natural strength of girls, but this still must be nurtured and strengthened. It's not a matter of being self-conscious or deliberate— that would actually get in the way— you just go with the flow. Your baby calls you, you respond. It's casual, natural, and soothing for you both.

Growing the Prefrontal Cortex

The first six months of little Lucy's life are rather sleepy, as she just gets used to being out in the world. In the second six months, things speed up. Just inside her little forehead is an area of the brain that, if you could see it, looks like a cauliflower, wrinkled and furrowed. This area, known as the *prefrontal cortex* (PFC), is now starting to grow. The PFC is the most complex part of the brain, and it governs some things that are very important for life. The prefrontal cortex is the seat of empathy, sociability, and human contact. It's what makes us human.

The prefrontal cortex couldn't grow earlier, because it would have made Lucy's head too big to be safely born. And what's in there, the software, also needs to be programmed by Lucy's parents or caregivers, because they are unique to her family and culture and will help her live with them for the many years it will take to raise her.

Along with its social functions, the prefrontal cortex also controls two important abilities:

* The ability to focus, to pay attention.
* The ability to calm yourself down.

Babies can't calm themselves for one important reason: they are wired up for panic. In the wild (the way we used to live for a quarter of a million years), babies were carried about for most of the day because that was the best way to keep them safe and give them good care. And often the adults were walking for much of the time, so it was just a practical necessity. (Even today, in the so-called undeveloped world, babies are rarely put down. They also rarely cry.) In our long prehistory, there were plenty of predators about that would love to snatch a human baby for their dinner. So if a baby found herself alone or, worse still, a big hairy muzzle suddenly appeared in her face, dripping saliva—and it wasn't Dad—she was probably in trouble. Babies who cried loudly were more likely to be rescued fast. So fearfulness and noisy panic had a survival value that became part of our design.

This alarm system in babies left alone has a very important message for us as parents. For just as we are told right from birth to keep babies *warm*—since they can't regulate their own temperature—we also have to keep them *calm* because they can't regulate their emotions. So dozens of times a day, a baby gets upset, whimpers, or cries, and her mom, dad, grandparent, or sibling picks her up, soothes her,

What Is Calmness?

Calmness is not a character trait, it's simply a skill. You have to decide that it matters, that the quality of your presence would be better if you slowed yourself down and were really connected to people and the moment you are living in. Then you practice until gradually it becomes part of you. It benefits everyone around you—they feel peaceful and happy in your presence. It's exactly what children need in a parent. And it benefits you—with less stress hormones, you live longer and feel better. Calmness is well worth cultivating.

Calmness is made up of certain actions: breathing deeper, dropping your shoulders, settling your muscles, feeling your feet strongly planted on the ground, focusing your thoughts on the job at hand in a steady, easy way, and not going off into panicked thoughts. Even just counting three or four breaths, in and out, will slow your heartbeat and calm your mind down. Calm people are actually doing these things automatically; when an emergency strikes, they intentionally calm themselves *more* in order to counter the tendency to panic and do the wrong thing.

Self-regulating your level of emotional arousal is an incredibly valuable skill for life. All you have to do is notice, am I calm? If not, breathe a couple of times consciously, feel your feet on the ground, and notice how, as the last burst of adrenaline clears away, the calmness response starts to kick in. Practice this for a few days, and soon the natural appeal of calmness will pull you more and more to that peaceful and steady place. Everything is better—the taste of food, the scent of flowers, the feel of the warm water in your shower on your skin. You will find that time slows down, and you can think more in the pause before you open your mouth. And that has *real* benefits!

and helps her relax. "It's okay, everything's fine. There, there." Gradually, this soothing becomes part of her, she learns how to do it herself, but this takes several years of receiving the gift of calmness from others. It's all gradually building into strong mental health for a lifetime.

The Gift of Calm

Your little girl learns calmness for life from the ease and comfort you bring to her early months and years. (Even in the womb, your adrenaline crosses over into her body, so a calm pregnancy can pay off in terms of giving you a more restful and happy baby.) This means planning as much as you possibly can to spend the time before and after her birth and right into the first year or two with reduced pressure and the luxury of time with your little one.

This is so different from our idea of how to live: rush, hurry, and being busy are the keystones of modern life. But our babies are Stone Age babies, and modern madness does not serve them well. If you possibly can, make this time a break from the rushing world you may have lived in all your life.

Crying and Sleep

Feeling okay in the world is the first lesson you teach your baby girl. "You are loved and precious, I am here for you, and everything is okay." A frightened or lonely baby won't learn to calm herself if she is just left to cry—this is a common misunderstanding. She will go quiet eventually, but this is because of another survival pattern. "Nobody is going to come!" A baby's prolonged cries "in the wild" might attract danger, so if her cries are not successful after a few minutes, the baby shuts down and becomes physiologically "depressed." If parents are unresponsive—through suffering untreated postnatal depression, or being drunk or stoned, or just not

The Hormones of Love

Many of us today feel unprepared for parenthood. A hundred years ago, most families had seven or eight children and their homes were noisy and crowded places, but often very happy ones. Everyone grew up with babies and toddlers around them and knew how to handle them. Today it's very different. One study found that one-third of new parents have *never* held a baby before they get their own!

Luckily, our hormones help with this inexperience. New mothers' bodies flood with a hormone called prolactin. If you are lucky and can breastfeed your baby, then prolactin levels go much higher in your bloodstream and make you feel dreamy and slowed down. It helps you to focus and be there for your child. Other hormones help, too; when you hug your baby, or your partner or a friend hugs you, the hormone oxytocin (the love hormone) makes you feel contented and settled.

Oxytocin is a remarkable hormone; it is released when we have an orgasm; it is released when we greet a friend; and when we eat food with someone, sitting together at a table, it increases in our bloodstream. At birth, if it's a relaxed environment, and we feel safe, it floods into us. You need all the oxytocin you can get! When people talk about bonding, it's oxytocin at work. People who did not get enough love, and therefore enough oxytocin, often can be found seeking that satisfaction in other ways—through fame, doing drugs, compulsive sex, shopping, stuffing our face with unhealthy food. Or writing books!

Gabor Mate, famous for his work with drug addicts on Vancouver's East Side, says that heroin, and the rush of well-being as the injected drug surges into your bloodstream, is a substitute, a mimic, of being loved—but with a much different result.

It's all an attempt to get that oxytocin we didn't get in our mother's arms. So giving your baby lots of affection is a great liberator. It makes her strong and independent and a people person who will love and be loved for the whole of her life.

caring—and if this happens often enough, the baby decides that "my efforts don't have any effect on others." This pattern will become part of how she responds to difficulty in life. It is called *learned helplessness*.

It's not a pattern you want your child to have, because she will lack a sense of mastery or hope in difficult situations. "Depression" is often misunderstood—it is simply an ability of the human body to shut down, a holdover from ancient times when we had to sit out bad weather or endure long winters of cold and dark. At such times, with little food around and no energy to catch it, moving little, eating little, and doing little was the best way to survive. But the depression response can easily become overdeveloped. Teaching depression to a child by ignoring her is not going to help her. She may lie still, but she is actually very unhappy.

There is a middle road here, especially when getting babies to sleep, which can be an important part of parents' survival. Sometimes a baby in her crib will make sounds, trying to bring the adults to play with her after she's been put to bed. It's fine to let her whimper and whine a little as part of her giving up on "game time" and letting sleep take over (especially when mom or dad is totally exhausted and just needs a rest), but if the whimpering turns into full-voiced distress, that's not good. She needs calming and settling. The caring bond between you is endangered, and she needs to know you are there. (In the Author's Notes, on page 201, you will find some good reading suggestions on how to get more sleep for your baby, and for you, without using harsh methods to do so.)

You Also Have to Excite Your Baby!

After all this talk about calmness, it's important to remember the opposite message, too: we don't *always* want our babies calm. Babies and toddlers also need to learn to go into higher states of excitement, to increase their emotional range and enjoyment. From time immemorial, parents and siblings will just naturally tickle, tease, excite, and stimulate babies. Your little girl will giggle and "come alive"

How to Play with a Baby

With your baby daughter, even from the very first weeks, playfulness can be at the heart of everything you do. This playful mood delights her, but it also makes ordinary tasks so much easier if she sees them as fun.

For instance, babies have to be bathed. Some parents just hurry through this briskly, but most moms and dads can't resist the urge to make it a pleasure for their baby and themselves. They make sure the room is warm; they aren't upset about a bit of splashing; they swish the water around their baby, singing or chatting and making noises and, most pleasurable of all, lifting scoopfuls of water and pouring it down her back or front, which she just loves. Many of us can still remember this from our childhood, the delight of warm soapy water on our skin and a kindly person patting us dry with a soft towel.

At six months of age, when she can sit up, your daughter will pour water herself, squeeze a trickle from the washcloth, and pop soap bubbles. Bathtime can be a wonderland for her senses.

Even getting dressed, or having a diaper changed, goes better if done in a playful mood. Your daughter will fuss less because she associates this as a happy time. She will take all her cues from you; if you are stressed, she will fuss because she is worried about you. If you are happy, she will be, too.

When you play with a child, you are starting something big. Child-development experts are now convinced that playing is what brings out our brain's full potential. Play unleashes lifelong creativity. The greatest discoveries have been made by playful minds being inventive and different.

A girl raised with a sense of fun will not be shy or dull, she will "think outside the box" and bring this ability to whatever career she chooses. She will be able to get along with others in a happy way, because play is all about collaboration. Playfulness makes you confident and light-hearted, willing to try new things. It dispels stress and boosts your immune system. It makes you more active, which then promotes fitness and health.

If you aren't a naturally playful person, *just try it!* Play is as infectious as a baby's laugh. You will soon find your daughter's delight and natural capacity for fun captivates, and you will both have a ball.

when you energize her in whatever way works for you—singing to her or playing peek-a-boo by hiding your face behind your hand or a magazine and popping out again. Tickles, cuddles, and dancing with her in your arms will help her coordination and body sense, but don't do it for that reason, do it for the fun of it. Put some music on, and let yourself go!

Even the rough and tumble play that dads do with small children helps this along. Dads are notoriously prone to exciting kids by tossing them about, chasing and wrestling, and swinging them around. Your daughter may get a little stressed by this, but if it is done in the right way (which you can tell by watching her face for signs of real distress, and backing off a little), she will get over it and start to giggle. Research has found that little girls who play with their dads

Our Baby Will Fit Right In (LOL!)

Have you ever talked with a young couple who doesn't have kids, but plan to?

Often couples in that first flush of confident planning, especially those who are very success driven, will proceed into parenthood full of goals and high aspirations. "We will never . . ." and "our child will . . . ." There's a lot of "will" and "won't" in their vocabulary, because before you have children, life actually sometimes responds to your intentions. You still have the illusion of control—something that real parents have long abandoned!

When talking to parents-to-be, it's important never to disillusion them. (You should never discourage the young!) A common claim of the not-yet-but-soon-to-be-childed is, "Our baby will fit in with our lifestyle. If it learns to fit in right from the start, it will be that way all along." Experienced parents listen to these plans and do their best to contain their mirth.

I had some friends who were talking this way. They were both nurses and had put off starting a family. Then when it came time to make babies, it took a while for it to happen. Finally they had their baby, and I didn't hear from them for a while.

Continued

At the time, I belonged to a trauma team, helping emergency service workers after especially stressful incidents. This work sometimes happened very late at night. One night driving home through town at about 2 a.m., I saw a strange hunchbacked figure shambling along the waterfront. There was a large lump on its shoulder, and it was clutching it and walking unevenly but resolutely along the deserted street. I have an active imagination, and I immediately thought—"It lives beneath the wharf! Creeping out at night to feast on pizza crusts, shunning the human gaze." But as I drew closer, I recognized my friend! The hump on his shoulder was a baby. He was walking the streets with his baby at 2 a.m.! He saw me and gave me two fingers and a grin—and I pulled over to see if he was okay. He just laughed as he read my thoughts: "This baby is fitting in with our lifestyle!" He was walking the baby to get it to sleep; it was the only thing that worked.

Take it from me, babies do not fit in with your life. Babies take the Kleenex of your life and roll it into a snotty ball! If you do parenthood even half well, it will rearrange your world. Babies do this in one especially important way (I'm not sure whether to whisper this or shout it, but here goes): *you* won't come first in your own life for at least twenty years. If you've spent twenty or thirty years being a self-centered so-and-so, you will find parenthood extremely challenging. But it will be good for you. Hopefully, parenthood and your child will reward you with enough love that you won't mind this, but it's important to know what you are in for.

(In our family, this was definitely how it was. As mentioned earlier, we planned carefully for homebirths with great midwives and doctors on standby, and both times we had emergency caesarians. But you claw back what you can—I was there both times, trying not to faint, and I held our babies the second they emerged from behind the green sheets. A few hours after my son was born, I faced down a monster nurse who wanted to put a two-foot plastic tube into his stomach for a sample "just in case." Our babies slept with me on the floor of the hospital room so that they were near their mom as she recovered from her operation. So I am not saying give up your ideals, but give up your well-planned perfect life, and learn to be flexible!)

Parenthood is so worth it, and so difficult, at the same time. Say good-bye to self-absorption. You never needed it anyway. It didn't look good on you.

when they are toddlers are much more stress-proof than those who had it all too safe and gentle!

(A cautionary note, especially for dads, when a baby is little, be careful with their necks—and their body generally. Babies cannot support the weight of their heads with their little necks for many months, and it may flex to the point of injury or sprain. Always support their heads and necks firmly as you move them around.)

There is something else even more important: setting an example of fun. Your daughter learns most by watching you. If you are happy, exuberant, silly, and fun with her at those times that it is appropriate (that is, not when driving the car), then her capacity for being happy will grow. If you are friendly to people you meet, enjoy getting your clothes on, sing while you shower, are kind to people in shops or in the street, speak well of people, get cross when you see something unjust or wrong, then your daughter will be taking in and making these attitudes her own, from a surprisingly young age.

It's worth checking up on this—especially for moms, who are the number one role model for their daughter's whole approach to life. Spend a day having a close look at yourself. *Do you frown, stress, grump, and hurry your way through life?* If that is so, being the mother of a newborn little girl might make you want to change that.

Don't Educate—Just Enjoy

In recent years, there has been an avalanche of products and programs—DVDs, flashcards, books, and expensive courses—to take advantage of parents' anxiety to have a smarter child. Despite all this effort and expense, with babies being urged to read at two or play the cello at four, there is absolutely *no* evidence that these approaches have any benefit at all. In fact, such educative efforts may have real costs, making parents and child more anxious and their relationship more strained. It's tempting to say that any product or place with the words "early learning" in its title should be avoided at all costs. I'm not saying that, but it's tempting!

Continued

Of course, babies and toddlers love stimulation, but it's how we go about it that matters. Studies of vocabulary acquisition (learning and using lots of words) have found something very interesting: kids do not get a larger vocabulary from being hammered with stimulating words and ideas. Researchers have found that the toddlers with the most words in their repertoire are the ones whose parents *listen* to them the most. It's not hearing lots of words, but using and enjoying them that fixes them in your child's memory. Children remember words when they experience the power of words to interest and engage others. "Give me the teddy, Daddy" (Father uses the teddy to tickle his daughter, making her giggle). "No, Daddy, give me the teddy *slowly*."

So we have to take the pressure out of parent-child relating. The very best thing you can do with your little girl is *enjoy* her. Chatter mindlessly to her—this really does come naturally if you let it. Singing and gooing and being funny with a baby (which is exactly what makes them prick up their ears, smile, or giggle) helps her attunement to language as an exciting tool that makes people do things. An uneducated rural mother in a developing country or a teenage mother with a good sense of fun often does a better job of this than someone with a degree in business administration—because she knows how to relax and enjoy.

What if being around babies doesn't come naturally to you? What if you had a chilly or distant and uptight childhood with parents who had those attributes, too? Playfulness may not come naturally at first, but it will happen, if you don't worry about looking or sounding silly (because that's the point). See what works to make your little daughter laugh and smile. She has a million years of mammalian history stored inside her, and, like any kitten, puppy, or wombat baby, she loves to do what develops her best—and that is *play*.

Not a second of babyhood is wasted. Babies are learning all the time, and we are their teachers. These early months can feel dreamlike and unproductive to parents used to achieving all kinds of goals, but it's actually the most productive time you will ever spend.

In a Nutshell

* Little Lucy discovers that the world is a good place because her parents can be trusted.

* Babies seek reassurance from us to manage their natural anxiety. We need to organize our lives so we can be calm and emotionally present, especially in those first six months.

* The second six months of life is when your daughter acquires the basis of all her people skills—the rhythm of interaction and how to be peaceful.

* Babies also need to be excited, played with, and awakened to the fun of life. Luckily, that's not so hard.

* Baby stimulation products and programs are usually a waste of money and may even just add stress to your relationship. Don't educate, just enjoy.

* Babies don't fit into your lifestyle, you have to fit into theirs. Prepare to have your life turned on its head. Accept this, and you will have a lot more fun and joy.

CHAPTER THREE

Learning to Explore (Two to Five Years)

One day your baby is on her feet, toddling, then suddenly nothing in your life is ever the same! No cat is safe, no goldfish, and no precious vase on a coffee table. (Though even crawlers could probably have put those at risk.)

A girl between two and five has one single purpose: to explore. This is the age when Girls Just Want to Have Fun. She does this with huge determination, and her will is strong. Being stopped annoys her greatly. Of course, sometimes she has to be stopped, but hopefully with distraction, or diversion, or sometimes with a cry of "hands off" along with a scowl. But in the main, exploring is what you *want* her to do and giving her lots to explore makes for a happier and smarter girl.

Because she *is* a girl, there are extra reasons why this stage matters; in fact, how you handle it is crucial. This is the time to give her the greatest range of abilities and areas of confidence that you possibly can. From nature to art to athletics, it all gets its start between two and five.

No Limits to Girlhood

Sometimes the limits we put on girls are totally unconscious. Just recently, a remarkable study was carried out into the way we talk to toddlers. It was discovered that without knowing it, parents talk with a different focus, and about different things, depending on the gender of their child.

If he's a little boy, they say,

"Look! There are *three* rabbits in the field over there."

If she's a girl, they say,

"Look at those *cute* rabbits!"

If it's a boy, they say, "Wow, you've made that tower *ten blocks high!*"

If it's a girl, they say, "What a *beautiful* tower you've made."

Can you spot the difference? Boys = numbers, girls = feelings. It's totally unconscious, but it has huge implications. And what else are we changing? Nobody really knows.

Does this matter? Well, it's long been known that even though girls are equally able at math, most boys *enjoy* math more and go further with this subject at school, and further into those careers that need some math (which includes a lot of the best-paid jobs). Girls are often quite frightened by math. (And to be honest, some girls are frightened by scary male math teachers, of whom there seemed to be a lot, at least when we were kids.)

I am sure that no parent ever sets out to disadvantage their girls around useful number skills, yet we unconsciously start making the boys practical and the girls emotionally focused.

So here's a suggestion: perhaps we ought to *reverse* this. Girls are well wired for being emotionally aware; we can encourage that, but we can also spice our chatter to them with lots of number stuff. "How many rabbits can you see?" And our boys are already wired for spatial knowledge, so "Those rabbits are nervous. Look, they've stuck their ears up to listen for us" can get them thinking about feelings. No need to get obsessive about it; I am willing to make a bet that just reading this has already got you thinking about what you say.

Talk to your toddler daughter about numbers and counting, and praise her for good engineering with her Lego bricks. Don't ever assume "girls don't . . ." anything, because they can, and they will, if we believe and encourage them early on. Sally Ride, the first American woman astronaut, dedicated her life after going to space to getting girls to study science. It creates more opportunities for them and doubles the talent pool of good scientists, which we definitely need.

Enthusiastic Learning

Because learning and fun are the same thing for a happy child, in the years from two to five your daughter will do more self-educating than thousands of dollars in school fees could ever buy for her later on. It's very sad when parents are too busy earning in the toddler years to have time to play and do things with their little ones. And it's pretty tragic if when those kids actually get to school, the love of exploring has died inside them.

Kids learn to love life and learning from the adults around them. On top of their natural curiosity, they will also follow ours and catch our enthusiasm. Watch an experienced mother or father on a bus with a toddler, and you will see that they point things out to them with feeling. If you are excited (or even pretend to be, just a little), she will catch your mood.

Think for a minute about your attitude to insects or nature in the raw. If you say, "Ick, horrible ants. Aargh, get away!" then, of course, your daughter will be scared of them, too. But if you say, "Wow, have a look at this," she will catch your attitude. It doesn't mean she should poke into spider's nests or pick up death adders, but you can teach her a sensible interest, and she will be fascinated for the rest of her life.

It's the same with machines, the insides of cars and computers, garden sheds, tools and making stuff, craft work, music making, art and sculpture, cooking, dancing, loving being in the forest or at the beach; these are all "caught" from the grown-ups around her.

Lots of Arty Stuff Is Free

The best learning aids for your two-to-five-year-old daughter are simple and cheap. Not fancy "educational" toys or gadgets that provide all the action with batteries or flashing lights; the simpler, plainer, and tougher, the better.

Arty kinds of activities are encouraged by having lots of recycled paper on hand, along with an abundant supply of pencils, crayons, and paints. Cardboard boxes, egg cartons, old greeting cards, and paper catalogues all lend themselves to creative playing and don't cost a penny. You can build up a considerable supply of creative materials in reserve for a rainy day or quiet time each day, and bringing out something new starts the process all over again.

But here's a hint—be sure to get these tidied away and orderly after each session, and get your daughter's help to do this. Then it's encouraging to start each new play session without having to wade through yesterday's mess. You can also alternate: crayons one day, paints the next, glue and tearing up colored paper another, so there is more sense of new adventures to be had.

Clothes

Girls should have plenty of old and tough clothes so they can be messy and happy in the dirt or doing art activities with paint, water, and glue and not freaking out about getting it on themselves or their clothes. In fact, little girls don't need fragile or fancy clothes at all. Those fashionable frilly numbers really have no purpose for little girls except to make them anxious about how they look. Fashion on children is for the benefit of adults, and if your child doesn't look cute enough already in a T-shirt and overalls, then you need to read fewer magazines. (There is nothing sadder than seeing a toddler dressed in such prissy and "feminine" clothing that she can't do anything but sit and be "good.")

One mom told me recently, "I used to say to my toddler daughter, 'That dress looks gorgeous' or 'How pretty you look.' But I have started to say, 'Let's put on these sneakers (or rubber boots) so you can run and play.'"

A Simple Environment Is Best

There is an important principle, discovered by psychologist Kim Payne, author of the wonderful book *Simplicity Parenting,* which is that a clutter of toys and materials actually makes for *less* play—it's all too much choice—whereas a few simple things, in a box ready for getting out, leaves more scope for imagination. If your child's bedroom is already awash with toys, quietly take away the less favorite ones, bag or box them for use another time. When your daughter looks at a sea of teddy bears, dolls, games, and bits of creation cascading all over the floor or all over her room, she feels the way you do—exhausted. And really, does anyone need more than two teddy bears? Well, okay, three.

Nature Is Essential

A backyard with real plants and soil, water, and maybe some trees is great. A rough treehouse (or even a big cardboard box) creates a base to play from and in. Backyards naturally come equipped with insects, lizards, and birds, though you can perhaps still add an old safe dog.

Girls need a chance to move around in nature. If you live in a block of apartments or have no yard, get to the park, countryside, or coast whenever you get the chance. Let them experience the rough textures and long-distance views, as toddler eyes need to look long distances and absorb natural sunlight to develop good vision. Running around on uneven surfaces will also make their legs flexible and strong. The sheer mystery of what's behind that bush or tall grass will help their imaginations, too.

Computers, iPads, and DVDs have their place, but for small children through to teens, these electronic devices can warp the senses and affect brain development negatively, because they are all flat and clean and the same distance away. You don't refocus your eyes or move about enough to develop the balance and activity centers of the brain. And you don't really feel love and connection to an animal on a screen in the same way as something you can touch and hug.

Matilda Learns Not to Be Fearful

(This story was told to me by my psychotherapy teacher, Bob Goulding, at the Western Institute in the 1980s. Bob was the grandfather in the story. He was a wonderful man.)

Two-year-old Matilda was enjoying playing around the swimming pool, carefully watched by her mom and grandparents. She would play happily in the toddler pool, but from time to time she would wander across to the deeper pool for a closer look. Suddenly, she simply stepped from the edge and completely disappeared into the deep water. Her grandfather, fortunately wearing some old shorts, jumped straight in after her. He grabbed Matilda immediately and pulled her out. Matilda, still utterly surprised, screwed up her face and was clearly about to start wailing. But before that could happen, her granddad did an interesting thing. Holding her at arms length, he shouted, "Wow! Matilda swims! What a great swimmer she is! You are great!" while laughing and looking very pleased. Matilda seemed to hesitate, look at him for a puzzled moment—he was hard to ignore—then she did a remarkable thing. She simply changed her face to a big smile and joined in the laughter.

Her mom came and took over, carrying Matilda back into the water and played with her, anchoring the experience into a positive one.

Would this turn Matilda into a risk taker? We don't think so; it was scary enough to have taken that sudden plunge, but the reaction taught her that adventures can be taken on the chin, and it's better to laugh than cry. In her brain, the pathways toward quick recovery and resilience were beginning to be put in place.

If we didn't have pool fences, it might make sense to terrify kids about water. (Aboriginal parenting traditionally involved terrifying children about monsters that lurked beyond the firelight at nighttime, because it *was* important they didn't stray. In my Yorkshire childhood, we were half-laughingly warned about the Bogey Man.) Helping our daughters to see life as an adventure and to be confident in their own skills and judgment is important because it means they can live a *larger* life. These will be the girls who scuba dive, volunteer for Doctors Without Borders, learn to pilot a plane, or play gypsy violin in an indie rock band. Although, I am trying to talk you *into* this!

If Matilda's mom or dad had freaked out, started yelling and carrying on after Matilda's unexpected dip, this little girl would have added to her own already considerable startle that the parental message was that water is scary. She may well have become phobic of water and swimming itself as a result. "Hell's bells," she thinks, "even Mom and Dad are terrified!"

The direct teaching that her grandfather offered—"Look here, this is fun!"—can be applied to many things in life, and from a very early age. We can help our daughters to be comfortable with animals, nature, climbing, books and libraries, sporting exertions, people, the night sky, the ocean, the list goes on. And they will carry this love of the world into their lives forever. Whenever you show her a new experience, you can add some enthusiasm, some "Hey look—isn't this great?" so that she also takes in a positive message.

Be sensible about it, but see if you can extend your daughter's boundaries every chance you get.

Three Should Be Free

With girls of age three or four, the goal and need of her brain is to play, to not be pressured, and to be able to be creative and free. These qualities will one day make her a great scientist, boss, artist, problem solver, or friend. She will always want to and be able to "do her own thing." But if she is made to perform—by a preschool with "early learning goals," or a parent who wants her to play violin, or some activity that grooms and preens her for adult consumption (participating in child beauty contests are a stunningly awful example), then she will not develop properly, will be cramped and tense, and lack creativity. Whole nations have experienced this through overdemanding schooling for the under-sixes. The result is a total lack of creativity, a population that is cowed, conformist, and compliant. By six or seven, a girl is ready for some (not too much) serious learning imposed from the outside. Her brain has moved on to a whole different stage. If it comes too soon, though, it actually harms her intellect and her eventual ability to be talented and bright.

So think twice about structured or organized activities that involve any kind of performance or competition. These just take the joy out of something she would otherwise have loved. Activities where all the kids simply get into it together and learn happily at their own pace are much preferred.

A final note—the two to five years are exhausting, and you can be a bit isolated. Don't think you have to be an education ringmaster for your kids all day. They need to occupy themselves, dream and dawdle as their imagination grows. It's in the gaps and quiet times that children do their growing. Turn off TVs and radios so they can think and talk internally, which they love and need to do as they play.

Don't let yourself get lonely, either. Join a playgroup, where the kids start to have fun with others, and you get to be with other moms or dads (there are dads' playgroups, too, now). Also learn to be boring sometimes and encourage your kids to just play around and without you while you merge into the furniture. You need your rest.

Choosing Toys

If you have heard *anything* about getting girls off to a good start, it's probably been about "gender-stereotyped toys." The role of toys in widening, or limiting, your little girl's play choices is a huge thing, and you'd think by now companies would have really gotten past this. But here's the bad news: it's getting *worse*. Companies never give up on trying to hook kids and parents with heavy marketing—especially on TV, where toys can be made to look so much better than they really are.

This article is by Paula Joye, a journalist and fashion columnist, website publisher, and a very sensible mom. I couldn't put it better.

Role Model or Pole Model? by Paula Joye

My youngest daughter is five and spent the weekend penning a Christmas Wish List to Santa. Nestled between a backpack shaped like a koala and a detective magnifying glass is a request for a Bratz Masquerade toy. She saw it advertised while watching *Finding Nemo* on television. The doll is dressed in an outfit that would look great wrapped around a pole. She has swishy, knee-length hair with pastel streaks, hoop earrings, and more black kohl eyeliner than a Kardashian.

I'm a little stuck because we don't have any Bratz in our house. I'm not sure exactly what I don't like about them. I loathe the lollipop heads and cushion pouts. Hate the heavy makeup. But I think what upsets me the most is their wardrobes. Seriously, these dolls wrote the rules on Red Light. A toy designed for five- to ten-year-old girls shouldn't be so overtly sexy. Pretty, geeky, smart, ugly are all fine but scantily clad dolls should be reserved for lonely grown men who can't get real girlfriends.

For me the message is just too narrow. The Bratz brand is thirteen years old, which means the original crash-test consumers are just starting to flex their fashion chops. On the weekend, I watched some of these girls heading into the Eminem concert in Sydney. They were wearing clothes that defy description.

Mainly because there was so little fabric covering their bodies that I'm struggling to come up with words other than naked and nude to describe how they looked. This is the first batch of young women to have been influenced by a society hell bent on fast-tracking them into womanhood, and the first place we're going to see the results is in the fashion choices they make. What struck me more than the bare skin was how homogenized their look was. Everyone was dressed identically. It was a sea of tiny, cut-off denim shorts and crop tops. Teenagers have always copied one another—it's normal to dress the same way as your friends—but there used to be so much more diversity and self-expression. I remember copying the wardrobes of Madonna, Wendy James, and Diane Keaton at the same age. I experimented all the time. But there was none of that in this crowd. It was Same. Same. Sexy. Same.

We can't blame this on Bratz or Barbie alone—there are so many influences that play on young girls—but it does make you despondent about the serious lack of role models both on the toy shelf and in the mainstream. Once they wave bye-bye to Dora and Angelina, the choices are whittled down to Bindi Irwin, Harry Potter's Hermione, and a couple of exceptions on Nickelodeon. Otherwise it's Miley, Taylor, Selena, and The Biebs. Where are Pippi Longstocking and Nancy Drew? Why isn't there a Kate Winslet for tweens?

It would be so easy for me to capitulate on the Bratz present. Seeing her little face light up when she opens it on Christmas morning is a tempting trade. But every time I teeter, I close my eyes and visualize her dressing the doll up in its miniature thigh-high boots, a micro-mini skirt, and green boob tube and . . . well, I want more.

More imagination from the toy manufacturer, more depth from the doll, and frankly a little bit more fabric for my money.

Finally, no toy advice would be complete without a word about Lego. There is no doubt about it, Mr. Lego, if there was one, was a genius. He deserves a Nobel Prize. There is no construction toy that comes close in its almost planetary popularity, usefulness, and

Blank and Unbranded

There is something really important to say here about dolls. At Waldorf schools, where kids are rarely rushed and a lot of thought goes into stages and ages, they have dolls with no faces. These toys are just blank and plain, with perhaps some simple clothes. The amazing thing is—kids love them. What happens is that the child at play puts all her own imagination into the feelings the doll might have, what it might look like, and what it does.

The doll doesn't program the child. These dolls are the ones taken to bed at night with them, tucked in, and used to play out all their dreams, imaginings, and fears. It's the very opposite of a Bratz doll. For little children, boys and girls, the less corporate their toys, and the more natural and unbranded, the better.

general magic. It can stimulate minds in different versions from babies to tech-headed teens—and it benefits and is loved by girls just as much as boys, given the chance.

But recently Lego got kidnapped by the marketers, who decided a girls' version was needed. Listen to what they came up with: five curvy little friends who bake, home-make, decorate, hair style, and shop! Anything gender-limiting in that little selection?

Boys' Lego, on the other hand, is about firefighting, space exploration, knights in armor, buildings, cars, houses, furniture, and *any-thing* you want to make it. Boys play in Lego World, whereas girls play in their own little ghetto called Heartlake City! (No firefighters or policemen there, they have to get the boys over if the beauty salon catches fire!) Naturally, when this new product line came out, women rose up in outrage. One angry writer summed up this in one neat sentence. "There *is* a girls' version—it's called . . . Lego."

There's no doubt Lego did their research, spending millions and taking years. Their head researcher told a Danish newspaper that they found that girls had a single overwhelming preoccupation— with *beauty*. That's what the new girls' Lego was built around. Girls wanted to project themselves into dolls who were being, or getting made, beautiful. Now I am not arguing with their finding, but that's a measure of how *damaged* girls are now. "How do I look?" is their strongest interest. If you want this to be your daughter's preoccupation, then girls' Lego is for you.

So by all means get your daughter Lego, but not the girls' version. Not the pink and purple beauty salon or the café. Sure, she might build those of her own choice, but she might prefer rockets, castles, cannons, horses, trees, trucks, and farms.

Making Her Strong, by Shaaron Biddulph

Raising a Strong Girl Starts Young

If you are lucky, you will know some strong women. They stand up for themselves and other people. They don't quit under stress. They are people you want on your side when the going gets tough. How did those women become strong? Were they born that way? Usually the answer is no; they became strong because they *had to*.

Some girls growing up have to face enormous adversity and hardship, such as the illness of a parent, a death, or an accident, or having to leave one's home country because of war or persecution. These women, with a combination of outer support and inner resources, often discover a strength inside themselves.

Most of us take smaller steps through life and gradually grow strong. We go to a new school where we don't know anyone, we face needles and blood tests at the doctor's, we stand in front of a classroom or an interview panel, we keep our commitments even when we are tired or sick. Gradually, life teaches us that we can get through things.

But there is a third way—one which is safer and probably the best. We can be *raised* to be strong. We can help our girls get there, and a big part of parenthood is doing this—not by mistreating them or making them hard, but by helping them kindly to handle tougher and tougher things.

Seeing Things Through

It begins with learning to help and be a part of the family team. How you do it has to be appropriate and right for the age of your child.

* With toddler Matilda, her mom always has a bedtime routine. She has a bath, does her teeth, then tidies up her things before a story in bed.

* With preschooler Amy, her mom expects her to help clean up after dinner by bringing the plates to the dishwasher, then putting away her toys, and putting her dirty clothes in the laundry basket.

* School-age Mandy looks after the dog, gets its food and water, brings it in at nighttime, and walks it with her dad a couple of times a week.

* Teenage Erin goes to her job at the library three nights after school to earn money for the school trip.

* University student Myriam cooks the family's meal on the three nights a week when her mother and father both work late.

While it takes a bit of time to get kids doing things for themselves, it really pays off by the time they are at school or become teenagers. By then, they will naturally feel capable and know they are indispensable to their families.

Getting Your Daughter to Cooperate

When we tell a toddler to do something, sometimes she obeys, often she doesn't. Start with a simple request and engage with her as you make it, looking her in the eye. If she doesn't get started, give her a sterner warning. Sometimes that works. When it doesn't, we have to follow through.

Some people yell or threaten, or else give up and let it drop. Neither teaches a child very much.

Imagine your child has done something "naughty"—disobeyed, hit somebody, broken something in a tantrum, drawn all over the bathroom with felt pens. In that situation, we would take them to a place that's away from distractions—a corner, a wall, a nook somewhere—and tell them to stand there and talk to us. If they don't cooperate, we tell them to stay there until they can. (With a really feisty toddler, you might have to carry them there, or hold them there.) Wait until they say they are ready to deal with you.

Continued

With three-year-old Zara, the interaction goes like this.

Parent: "Are you ready to talk?"

Zara: "Yes." (Mumble, grumble . . .)

Parent: "Tell me what you think you did that was a problem."

Zara: "Nothing."

Parent: "Do you need more time to think about it?"

Zara: "I hit Elly."

Parent: "Yes. That's right. You shouldn't hit people."

Zara: (Mumble, grumble . . .)

Parent: "What are you saying?"

Zara: "She had my dolly."

Parent: "Well, we can talk to her in a while. But this is about not hitting. What are you going to do to fix it?"

Zara: "I want a drink of water."

Parent: "Right now we are fixing what you did wrong."

Zara: "I'm sorry."

Parent: "So are you wanting to go and say sorry to Elly?"

Zara: "Yes."

Parent: "And what will you do differently next time?"

Zara: "Not hit Elly."

Parent: "Great! You figured that out really well."

Some people think discipline is about "winning" or "beating" your child, but that's not the goal. You actually want to make them stronger—to help them be clearer about how to handle themselves, their emotions, and be able to think really well even when they have strong feelings. (You can read more about this "stand and think" method in our book *The Secret of Happy Children*—it applies equally to girls and boys.)

Teaching Her to Get It Right

There is a lot of helping and teaching in discipline—it's not about conflict. When something isn't working or an opportunity comes up, you simply move into showing her how to go about behaving differently.

Let's say Lily has started screaming loudly at her brother to give her a turn on the slide. Lily is two, her brother is six. Her mom takes her away for a second to calm down.

Then she says, "Come with me. Let's try it again."

They go over to her big brother who is still on the slide.

She crouches down and asks Lily to say, "Please can I go on the slide, Jake?"

She says it for her, so Lily knows what to do.

Then she coaches her to do it herself, politely but clearly.

The next time, when she comes to complain, we check with her: "Did you speak up loudly and clearly and politely to your brother?"

Of course, you will also be talking to her brother about sharing and encouraging his little sister to play. He might be a few years older, and for him the lesson is how to get along and have more fun by cooperating. Lily's lesson, though, is just, "Ask, don't scream!"

There's always a sequence in teaching a child:

Do it for them.

Do it with them.

Watch while they do it.

Let them do it themselves.

It's All About Understanding Needs

Everyone has needs. Lily needs to notice that screaming doesn't work, and it just makes everyone annoyed with her. She needs to learn to use words clearly and well. For a toddler, that's a big step. Her brother (at six) needs to be able to listen, explain, share, and understand that toddlers have less patience. And you as her parent need to be able to preserve your hearing and peace of mind—toddlers shriek very loudly unless taught not to.

With little children, this teaching is done "live" and on the spot; by the time the teens come along, it is done in discussion away from the situation. It's more about rules and consequences. Teenagers might need to make it up to the person they hurt, or suffer the loss of some privilege, or rebuild trust by proving they can stick to what they have promised.

A Positive Mood

Often in our own childhoods, people disciplined with a lot of yelling or blaming. It was angry and unpleasant. Real discipline isn't like that. You need to do it with patience and encouragement. You have a dual aim all through this: that your daughter will become independent, which is what you want and they want, too; and that one day you will be great friends because you helped to get them there in good faith.

When It Counts

The aim of discipline isn't to have compliant kids. The aim is that when you are not there, or long gone, they will have inner backbone and be able to be strong and self-believing. One day, it's almost certain, your daughter is going to be somewhere late at night where people have been drinking. Someone is going to want them to go somewhere else in a car. They will be drunk or stoned beyond belief, everyone will be laughing, and her friends will be saying, "Come on, let's go."

She will reach inside herself and find some backbone. She'll say, "I don't want to go with him. He's drunk." Or, "Come on guys, I want to stay alive. Let's go back inside and call a cab."

In our work, we've talked to kids who are paraplegic or brain injured or had friends die in a car, or were raped after going with strangers to somewhere far from help. Inevitably they say, "I didn't think anything bad would happen" or, essentially, "I was confused and didn't take charge of myself." Discipline teaches you to think well under pressure and to speak up for yourself. It teaches you how to have boundaries, how to be strong.

If you can say to your child, "I'm not comfortable with that," and "That's wrong," then they will be able to use those very same words one day in a situation where they really need to. It's a very great gift that every young person needs.

In a Nutshell

* The years from two to five are for exploring. Give your daughter lots to explore, make, and do. Add your enthusiasm and energy to show her it's okay to be messy, into everything, and playful.

* Have lots of cardboard, paper, paints, and crayons around the house.

* A backyard really helps, and being in nature is vital.

* Dress her in clothes that are tough and damage proof so she is free to be herself.

* She might be destined to be an athlete, scientist, artist, or engineer—encourage whatever she shows an interest in.

* Don't have too many toys, and simplify her play space to make it more inviting.

* She might be nurturing by nature, or not. Simple blank dolls or teddy bears are enough to stimulate this side of her, and she can make up her own games.

* Avoid toys that tell your daughter it's all about looks and clothes. In fact, avoid anything aimed just at girls. The world does that quite enough already.

* Disciplining girls, kindly but firmly, ensures they will grow a backbone and be able to be competent and strong when it counts.

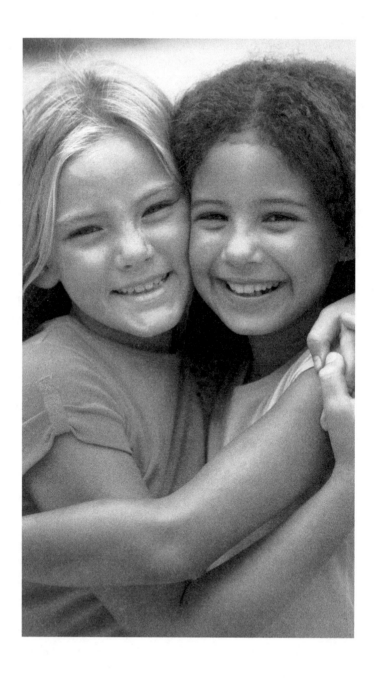

CHAPTER FOUR

Getting Along with Others (Five to Ten Years)

Making Friends

Friends are important to most of us, but for girls, they are like the oxygen they breathe. At age five or six, when most girls go to school, friends are who they rely on for company, comfort, and fun. Parents of daughters sigh with relief when their daughter finds a friend or two that she can really count on.

Of course, friends can also be a source of pain. Nine times out of ten, if your daughter comes to you in tears it will be because of something going on in her social world. (Boys seem so much more relaxed about it all. A small boy can fight with a friend—and I mean, really *fight*—but be best friends again an hour later. Some girls can still be worried on Friday that someone frowned on Monday, and they don't know the reason why!)

The fact is, human relationships are so complex that it takes decades to learn how to get them right. You and I are still learning. So your daughter will need your help. As her main anchor back at home, you will find yourself helping her to figure out "what went wrong," salving wounds, reassuring her, and sending her back out there to try again. Getting along with people is one of the most important things we help our kids to learn. Nothing has more effect on their future happiness and success at life. In this chapter, we'll help you understand the skills of friendship, so you can teach her.

How Friendship Grows

Babies are fascinated by other babies, but they don't really play together—Mom and Dad are just so much better fun. In toddlerhood, though, a child in a playgroup will often fix on another child with great intensity and will shower affection on their chosen target, who may have no say in the matter! Under-threes can't actually cooperate with each other for more than a few minutes (at least, without a referee), but they have at least noticed each other. The journey to friendship has begun.

By age four or five, most girls can play together well. What they most enjoy is imaginative play—games of make-believe. It's astonishing how much of a magical world they can dream up, with very little in the way of props. New Zealand's much-loved performers, the Topp Twins, were interviewed recently about their childhood on a 1950s dairy farm. They didn't have a lot of toys—but each had a sturdy stick, polished from long use, with a piece of rope tied to one end which served as the reins—because these sticks were their horses! Their dad would send the pair up to the back paddock to check a water trough, gravely advising them to "ride" to save time. And they always tied their steeds to the railing when they got home.

Make-believe isn't just about passing the time; it is the basis of all creativity—without it there would be no books, movies, music, or science. Nothing happens that isn't imagined first. Your daughter's playing happily by herself, or with friends, is the greatest brain development activity she will ever have.

Playing *together* involves a whole new set of skills. A girl playing on her own can call the shots because her teddies are not going to argue back. But to play together, children must negotiate a *shared* fantasy world—you can't be the queen of the pirates without a crew. If you are too much of a control freak, they will mutiny and sail away. Sneak a listen to girls at play and half of the time it's negotiation over who gets the plum roles!

Play is where we learn to relate to one another. In his book *The Wonder of Girls*, Michael Gurian tells a story about taking his daughters to the park. They are seven and four, and have brought their soft-toy animals along with them. It's early, and there is no one else around. The girls commandeer the big wooden pirate ship in the center of the playground and settle into an engaging game.

Suddenly a mom arrives with two boys. The boys are about the same age—he guesses five and eight. The boys noisily rush onto the boat. Their loudness and shouting disrupts the quiet play of the girls and their animals, and the girls stand off to one side, unsure what to do. They make a few attempts to restart their game, but the boys' domination of the space makes it hard to do.

Gurian is a boy expert, and he tries his best to be understanding, but he is quite angry. It's a real feminist moment (you'll notice my use of the word "domination" in the paragraph above). A high horse begs to be mounted here, but as he watches, unsure what to do, something interesting happens. His older daughter—the alpha girl—says something to the alpha boy. She and he do some pointing. She speaks to her little sister, who takes a toy over to the younger boy, and they position it on the prow of the boat. Within seconds, the four of them have begun an involved and interesting game featuring "princesses, giants, treasure . . . and Cinderella's lost shoe." It goes on for ages, and they have a great time.

The boys were not intentionally dominating, though that's not beyond boys to do by any means, they were just being energetic. It had a displacing effect on the girls, though. Left to themselves (that is, without adult intervention), the girls made their move, not to fight but to integrate with the boys, to not just "share the space" but share their minds as well. A game developed that was more fun than either pair would have had, the girls' imaginations and the boys' passion blending in a way that bodes well for all their futures.

When Things Go Wrong

Parents only need to get involved when nothing else seems to work. A discussion with your child that begins with their tearful complaint that "nobody will play with me" can lead to working out—well, how did it go wrong? You can talk to her about the "sharing of importance" and letting others have some say in the game.

It can get very intense. One of the shocking things, to parents as well as to children themselves, is how rough and heartless kids can sometimes be. But it's simply that they haven't learned to mask their emotions. They can hate fiercely, but briefly, and then all is forgiven. We shouldn't get involved unless violence threatens or someone comes running to get us. Even when that happens, try to avoid taking sides, but give them a chance to chill out and recover their poise. They will usually bounce back, and the game will have moved on.

By late elementary school, girls' friendships start to deepen into real emotional sharing. They will usually have one special friend, or perhaps a trio who get along well and are quite inseparable. The reason for this deepening of friendship in the pre- and early teens is that friends are part of the long journey away from depending just on Mom and Dad. As we become adults, we don't so much become independent, we just depend on a wider group of people.

In girls, this is revealed in their sharing of secrets. Under fives will tell everything to anyone, and can be very embarrassing at times, but from five to ten most children are intensely loyal to their families. In therapy, a girl of this age will rarely speak about her mother's drinking or her father's anger, for example. She needs her family so much that she feels drawn to protect them. But around the age of ten, girls begin to stand away from their family and see it in a clearer light. By midadolescence, girls will confide to a friend their deepest concerns and problems with their family. This can be a much-needed source of comfort and support since there is often some healthy and necessary conflict with parents at this time. Just as we comforted them about their friends in elementary school, their friends comfort them about *us* in high school.

Unlikely Friends

Sometimes girls will make unlikely friends. Play expert and psychologist Michael Thompson describes a classic case. A fashionable and cool twelve-year-old girl whose parents are going through a messy divorce makes friends with a studious and less sociable girl, who is steady and caring. Together they play games about cabins in the forest, horses, and princesses. For the cool girl, it's a huge relief to be able to still be a child with a patient friend who doesn't care about fitting in, boys, or clothes. Her fashionable friends are totally bewildered, but the differences enrich each girl and give them each a wider possibility of who they can be. Complementary friends—who are different in a way that balances the different strengths of each other—offer much more than being with girls who are all the same. Even for a short time, they bring benefits and growth.

Sharing problems is part of bonding—to such a degree that quite secure girls will make up problems ("OMG, my parents, they just *baby* me so much!") to be able to show empathy for a friend who has real stress in her family.

Elementary school friends are for companionship and fun. In the teens, you can add to this that they need their friends as a sounding board and for emotional support.

What Are the Skills of Friendship?

Once again, friendship skills all begin in babyhood. The secure attachment of mother and baby lays the foundations for being trusting, being available to love and to have a closeness with others. If your daughter was close to you, she will know how to be close to others.

The girls your daughter tries to befriend will sometimes be from insecurely attached babyhoods—moms who were cold and indifferent or stressed and depressed—and these friends may bring these "issues" to their friendship role. An insecure girl may show this by being clingy and wanting to own and not ever share her newly made friend. Or she may be dominating and controlling—we have to do what I say and go where I choose. Perhaps she will overcome this if a secure friendship manages to grow, but often our girls find these companions all too much and flee. If your daughter is the insecure one, it might be that she needs more closeness and friendship from you before she is ready to feel safe with others of her own age. Mothers and fathers are their daughter's first friends.

The Same-Age Ghetto

When talking about girls' friends, we seem to automatically assume that means same-sex peers. We probably have school to blame for that, and also the disappearance of real community from the way we live. In the last fifty years, girls have often been reduced to just the nuclear family and their school classmates for their social options, but this is actually quite unnatural. Girls ideally also need friends who are young women, half a generation older, savvy and yet youthful enough to relate to them with understanding. They need older women in their sixties and seventies, too, grandmother figures, who offer a grounded, wise, and comforting presence. They also need smaller or younger children who look up to them, get cuddles from them, and give them a taste of the joys of nurturing and being depended on, to relieve them of self-obsession and too much inwardness. They need boys or men friends who have no partnering or sexual intent toward them, so that they can expand out of those anxieties and see themselves as more completely human.

The chance to make these kinds of connections arise from the sort of street, town, or household you live in, the choices that you as her parents make with regard to the social and recreational life you lead. (A bland suburban life without belonging and participating can be crushingly isolating and impoverished for growing kids.) Belonging to a church, sports team, community project, or activist group exposes her to friendships with people who barely give a thought to weight, fashion, or boys and yet are miraculously happy and alive! Daughters need to be among people who lift them up and need their contributions. This gives them a whole different kind of self-esteem.

Check on your own behavior—are you calm, grounded, and available for your daughter when you are together? Some daughters need more reassurance than others. Some moms (or dads) are erratic—extravagantly overinvolved one minute, distracted the next. Their daughters soon put up shields because this is just too hard to handle. But take heart, nobody is perfect, and just as with all her friendships, your relationship with your daughter is always an opportunity to learn how to iron out the bumps.

There are seven core skills involved in being a friend:

1. Enjoying the company of others—lightening up and treating company as a chance for fun. Many a girl has started out shy but, with gentle encouragement, has come out of her shell.

2. Learning to take turns and share—this means giving up some of what you want for the pleasure of being with someone else. Point out to her that you have more fun if you play together, but you have to give a little to make that work.

3. Being able to empathize—imagining how you would feel in your friend's shoes, and being happy for her when she "wins" or "stars" in the game. This is a more advanced skill, one that doesn't always come easily.

4. Being able to regulate aggression—not screaming or clobbering your friends when you disagree. Not storming off because you are losing the argument.

5. Apologizing when you are wrong or hurt a friend's feelings.

6. Being able to read emotions—seeing when someone is angry, sad, or afraid and adjusting your behavior accordingly. You can even teach this with drawings of smiley, frowny, teary, and shaky faces, helping your daughter recognize them, and applying this to situations when her friends have been upset.

7. Learning when to trust or believe someone, and when not to, and understanding that people can be deceptive for reasons of their own. Your daughter will be shocked and hurt when a friend lies or deceives her. You will need to comfort her and explain that some people have not learned the value of being trustworthy. Don't lose heart, just be a little careful.

Each of these issues will arise often in your daughter's day-to-day life. When she comes to you hurt or bewildered, you can pinpoint which skill is called for, listen to her feelings, but then talk to her about how that skill can be put into practice. It will take a few tries to get it right, so follow up with her over a few days or weeks. Even we adults often don't get these situations right, so have respect for the hugeness of what she is having to learn, and praise and affirm her for even small steps.

Be a Friendship Role Model

As with most skills in life, a role model is the very best kind of help you can be. If a girl's mom goes up and talks to people in social settings, shows interest, and chats animatedly with them, her daughter can see how it's done and also how it creates a good feeling. A mom who is grumpy and doesn't have time for people is not likely to have a daughter who has those skills. If you are naturally shy, though, or she is, don't push it; the first step is to be comfortable with yourself. Often dads have different social skills than moms, and a daughter can mix and match what she observes in her parents and other close family members.

Sharing and taking turns is usually learned by having brothers and sisters. If your daughter is an only child, you might have to teach this and practice it at home. Helping your kids get along at home, patiently but dedicatedly, insisting on respect, kindness, and sharing, and solving conflicts calmly, will greatly help them to transfer those skills to their wider lives at school and elsewhere. If she is rude to you, then she will be rude to others, who might be less tolerant. So working on respect will really benefit her.

Empathy is learned through the experience of others showing it to you. Use feeling words, let your expression match that of your daughter and try to sympathize with her—take time to hear where her heart is. You will see your daughter at a young age begin to do the same with her dollies and teddies, as she bandages them, comforts them, and so on. That's a good sign that she will be a caring friend in real life.

Your daughter's ability to speak up for her rights matters a lot. If you are able to stand up to people in shops or at home, and speak out when you are unhappy, she will learn how to do this. When she has trouble with friends at school, you can rehearse with her the sort of things she could say, and how to word her objections so that she can be direct and clear in her response to them.

If you are a gentle or quiet person, parenthood might call on you to be tougher. Watch the movie *Oranges and Sunshine*—the heroine of that film, social worker Margaret Humphreys, is a gentle soul who fights governments and church authorities for the rights of her clients because of the power of her empathy for them. You don't have to be big or loud to be strong, just be clear—and don't give up.

When conflict arises, between you and your partner, for example, notice if you get angry or loud. Your daughter needs to see how you can keep your cool in tense situations. If you lose it all the time, she might decide to be different. Or she might end up being just like you!

Finally, it's great to sit down with your daughter and talk about "what makes a good friend." Make a list of all the things she can think of. Write them down. Then you can ask:

* Does she think *she* is a good friend?
* Who is the best friend she has ever had? Why?
* Has she gotten better as a friend as she has gotten older?
* What are her challenges in being a good friend?

These are great things to raise her consciousness about.

Friends can be an enormous source of strength and well-being. The skill of strong close relationships is one of the most important things you can give your daughter. It's worth the time you spend talking and helping her. Long after you are gone, she will still be drawing on your kindness and patience in figuring it all out.

A Counselor Talks About Friendships and Girls

Johanna is a counselor in the primary grades of a big elementary school.

As a school counselor, I am usually called on when girls' relationships go amiss. In elementary school, this seems to peak in fourth grade, but can sometimes heat up in third grade and continue in fifth. It's good to put energy in at these times before it all revs up again in eighth and ninth grade! Sadly, isolation by exclusion, "death stares," giggles, and pointing are all everyday occurrences at school, usually because one or two of the girls are less happy in themselves and fall into these hurtful ways of behaving. All the girls need help to stand up to this and not become part of the problem. It's important that meanness isn't just allowed to keep on happening or a happy environment can soon be lost.

What works? Both preventively and as a response when things are getting a bit much, we have special get-togethers to discuss "being friends." We talk about the recipe for a good friendship, what we offer in a friendship, that we are all different, but all want to feel included and cared for.

These small circle groups are run by teachers sensitive to girls' relational dynamics (and who don't just write it all off as "girls' stuff"). Mean behavior needs to be directly discussed so that it's out in the open, and they know strategies to interrupt bullying or stop silly acts of hurt from happening.

Adults need to know and be part of what is going on with girls and their peers. We shouldn't say "that's their world," because it's unnatural for kids of the same age to be left to work it out for themselves, and it usually doesn't work.

Emily–Be My Shadow or Else!

Emily, age eight, doesn't want her friend Anna to play with anyone else but her. She accuses Anna of not really being her friend if she wants to play with someone else. Anna is anxious about telling Emily that she likes football and playing with a big group of children. She fears losing a friendship that she does enjoy for the most part.

What works? Posing the question: How can we make sure that everyone's needs are being met?

The girls, if given support to work through this, do come up with the answers and a good plan. In this case, the girls devised a roster that on Mondays and Wednesdays Anna would play football in a big group, and Emily and the other girls would understand that they weren't being rejected and that Anna still valued their friendship. On Tuesday and Thursday, Emily and Anna would spend time together playing handball.

Maya—The Unappreciated Matchmaker

In order to try to gain popularity, Maya, 10, spends her lunchtime running between groups of boys and girls discussing who likes whom and telling the rest of the class that this girl and that boy are girlfriend and boyfriend. The girl involved is mortified by this attention. She starts to not come to school some days. Eventually, her mother finds out the problem and talks to the class teacher. The teacher explains to the class that fifth grade is too early for girlfriends and boyfriends, and it's better to focus on friendships in general.

What works? The school counselor met with Maya. Through sensitive discussion, it emerged that Maya feels lonely at school and has difficulties maintaining friendships. She thought that this would be a way of being accepted by the other girls. They started to look at other ways of developing and maintaining friendships that would be more successful.

Alpha Girls

In any school, there is usually a group of alpha girls who are more confident and vocal. The other girls in the class tend to be more thoughtful and kind, and prefer to observe the world before jumping in with both boots. If teachers are not aware and connected to this dynamic, the alpha girls dominate, get the best classroom jobs, the starring roles in plays, and lobby the teacher for their preferred way of things to happen. They can make the other girls miserable and have unfair influence and power.

It is important that the teachers level the playing field and make sure that everything is equitable and no one is left out. They need to rotate roles and responsibilities and have activities that value different characteristics—such as being careful, quiet, or slow, as well as dazzlingly talented! Not everyone wants to be an alpha girl, but everyone wants fairness.

The Language of Feelings

Feelings, or emotions (we use the words interchangeably), are a compass for being around other people. We need to have two sets of skills: first, to read our own feelings and listen to what they are telling us; second, to read other people's feelings, so we know how to treat them, care for them, or even stay away from them.

If you understand the language of feelings, you can better pass on this knowledge to your daughter and make her confident and strong.

HOW FEELINGS WORK

Humans have hundreds of different feelings, but the main social ones are simple and easy. There are only four:

> fear
> sadness
> anger
> joy

These four "points of the compass" help us to know how to take care of ourselves:

> when we feel afraid, we get cautious
> when we are angry, we stand up for ourselves
> when we are sad, we go inward and reflect and may want to
> hold or be held by someone we feel safe with
> when we feel joy, we relax and celebrate and restore our spirits

These four feelings can mix and match like the colors we blend to get every shade of the rainbow, but usually deep down we have one feeling at a time, and it really helps to be able to know what it is, in ourselves and in others.

Most living creatures have feelings: bees get angry, fish know fear and dart away from danger. Further up the line, elephants and great apes grieve and mourn. We human beings have the most sophisticated and complex emotions, but they are still based on those basic four listed above.

Emotions are a strong "guidance system," like a GPS, which you can use to understand and help your child. Ask yourself, "What is she feeling?" (What does that expression, that action, those words, tell me about her inner state?) Ask her about her feelings, get her to name them, and let her tell you what is going on in her world. This can lead to uncovering the causes of those feelings, if you are patient and win her trust, and to talking through what to do. But the feelings always need to come first, and sometimes your daughter won't want anything more than to get it off her chest and she will feel better again.

FEAR—AND LISTENING TO YOUR INTUITION

Many years ago in the United States, a serial killer was finally caught after taking the lives of numerous young women. After his capture, the police made an amazing discovery—that dozens of girls had encountered him but not gone with him. Asked why, they said, "I had a bad feeling about it" or even, "I don't know. I just was uneasy to go with him." These girls listened to their body signals, and our bodies often pick up subtle clues that all is not right. These girls were saved by listening to their fear.

Girls are often programmed, and perhaps even have natural tendencies, to be helpful and compassionate. People wanting to exploit or hurt them will often try to play on their sympathy by telling them, "I am looking for my lost dog," or "I am feeling ill, can you help me?"

Listening to your own feelings and inner voice and trusting them, and valuing your own judgment when others might be saying something different, is a "strong woman" skill. Tell your daughter that she has this inner voice and teach her how to listen to it. Share examples from your own life. See if she can think of instances when she has heard that voice and it has taught her something.

It's a fine balance; you don't want to make her afraid of the world outside your door, just alert in the way that kids are all over the world in more uncertain environments.

Teach her in a calm, strong way and give examples in day-to-day life: "That person smiled with their mouth but not with their eyes." Girls can be observant and aware that people have all kinds of different motives, and if they don't feel right, they should get away fast.

Girls and Asperger's

Somebody who is disabled at reading feelings or understanding them (such as someone with Asperger' syndrome or a degree of autism) may find other people totally bewildering. They will keep talking to someone who is totally bored or be friendly and gushing with a complete stranger. They may not realize that someone, such as their own mother or sibling, is sad when it would be totally obvious to even a stranger.

Girls with Asperger's use more of their brain to think through this, and so are less often diagnosed than boys, who have more trouble hiding the problem.

Asperger's can range from slight to full-blown, so watch for signs that your daughter finds people bewildering and upsetting and just can't figure out what to do right, such as if she is inordinately anxious in situations that don't seem to warrant it, or if she seems forced and artificial in relating to people, when you know she is doing her best.

The solution is the same as with a girl who isn't on the autistic spectrum: to help her learn the language of emotion and, by logic and gradual experience, learn to be comfortable socially. It just might take more support and explicit explaining of things that other children might naturally know. Fortunately, children with Asperger's are often very intelligent and can bring their "computer" brain to bear on the situation. They can think logically about what to do and say in social situations and how to read the feelings of others. In fact, they sometimes become more sensitive and connected than people who merely do this on autopilot. Don't be shy to seek out professional advice about help and training for her to learn good strategies.

ANGER IS ABOUT BEING STRONG

Anger is also part of our protective system. Used properly, anger does not mean shouting, hitting people, or acting abusively, but instead is a strengthening feeling that you won't be pushed around. If your daughter reads the signs in her body—a heating up and tensing of muscles, clenching of jaw muscles, or a frowning feeling in her face—then she knows "I am being made to do something I don't really want," or "These people are saying or doing things just to be mean; I won't let them get to me."

The quickest and best use of anger is to voice it. Teach your daughter to say, "I don't like that" in a strong voice, to glare, and stick her chin out: "Leave me alone," or to walk away while staring at the person who has insulted her or hurt her. Actually practice this with her, coach her to look and sound tough. If it's a friend she is feeling annoyed with, she can say, "I don't want to do that," or "No, I won't" more gently, but meaning it, and perhaps having to repeat herself a couple of times—"I've said how I feel." Of course, if you, too, sometimes model these behaviors, she will simply imitate you when the need arises.

When our daughter started preschool, the teacher told us that she was the only girl who would play with the boys. We were proud of her because it showed she was adaptable and adventurous. We weren't sure what her secret was to enjoying the rough and tumble way the boys played, but on more than one occasion, walking from the parking lot to the leafy outdoor play area attached to the school, we heard her voice loud and clear: "I don't like that!" She was comfortable around the boys because she knew how to set them straight!

SADNESS IS REAL

Sadness is a quieter and more inward feeling. It is about making changes on the inside, whereas fear and anger are about doing things on the outside. When we feel sad, our primary need is to be understood. Comfort and the time to express sadness give your girl the space to let go of the loss or disappointment. Often as parents we can't bear for our kids to be sad, and we try to rush them out of it with food treats or attempts at humor. It is better to trust that sadness will pass if we stay connected and give it time.

There are often things in a girl's day that might make her sad; a friend has let her down at school, someone she likes is moving away, a teacher promises something but does not deliver, she sees an animal dead on the road or something awful on the news and it tears at her heart. We can't fix these things, we just gradually find a sense of perspective, and your daughter will have to make this journey, too. It is years long, and you can't rush it.

The world *is* a sad place, and children can cope with this if their feelings are simply allowed to be while we stay close by, sending the signal, "Yes, but you don't have to bear it on your own."

A Secret Word

From the age of five, sometimes your daughter will go to someone's house and be away from your immediate protection. You need to know she is safe. One strategy is to have a "secret word" or phrase that she can use when she calls you, one that lets you know she doesn't feel right, or that something is making her uncomfortable. You and she can memorize this word and its use, very seriously, for whenever it's needed. For instance, she can ask to phone you and say, "My shoes are hurting," or "I saw an eagle today" (a code word you make up together is best), which means "Please come and get me straight away."

You will probably never need this secret word, but if you do, it's very helpful. Even discussing this alerts her to the idea that some places and people don't feel right, and if you notice that, we will always rescue you.

JOY

Joy is something that we need to cultivate and celebrate. In other cultures, people know a happy moment when they see one, and grab it with both hands. Everybody's in the kitchen just hanging around? Turn up the music and dance. Pick your child up and twirl her if you feel like it. Hug often. Lie about in a blissful heap with your children on the couch. Be silly when out in the open. "Horse around" in parks and on beaches. Smooch your child or tickle her mercilessly when the impulse takes you. Buy ice cream. Sing in the car.

Celebrate events. Don't go in for lots of presents, go in for simple memorable good times. During the holiday season, enjoy your extended family and remember that there really *is* peace on Earth for 95 percent of the human race.

Teach your daughter to laugh, to dance, to be wild and free, so her capacity for joy expands and develops. It's the antidote to the necessary suffering that is also a part of life, and it ensures that happiness has a permanent place in her soul.

Avoiding Dud Friends

Your daughter will sometimes benefit from some direct advice about spotting and avoiding untrustworthy friends. For example, ask your daughter to:

Notice if you are changing yourself in order to keep a friend, doing things that you don't really like, that are not you, because it's what they want. If you do this at the start of a friendship, you may find you have to keep it up to keep them. It's probably not worth it, and better to not start. A real friend is someone who is happy to compromise or take turns.

Sometimes you can make a friend who is chronically crabby. You assume it's because of something you have done wrong, and find yourself often "dancing around" trying to fix it. A chronically crabby person is sometimes just made that way—it's her approach to life; it rarely changes, and it gets a lot of control. You will just end up being exhausted, so find happy friends instead.

Tend and Befriend

At the heart of our understanding of babies is a concept called *attachment*. This is the scientific name for the bond between mother and baby. Some babies attach securely to their moms, some do not. These patterns tend to persist into adult life—if we don't learn how to love as a baby, we might have trouble loving as an adult. Over about sixty years of attachment research, though, nobody asked the gender question: Is it different for boys and girls?

When they did, something surprising was found. Boys who were insecurely attached would avoid their mothers or not trust them. This was simple self-protection: "She's not there for me, so I won't invest my feelings in her." However, many of the girls responded differently. When their mother was depressed or distant or even when she was angry, these girls, barely out of babyhood, would *go closer* to their mother and try to comfort her!

On the one hand, this might seem very cute and has survival value if the mother can revive her spirits, but it also has long-term risks. When in danger or conflict, most people respond with what is called a "fight or flight" reaction, filling with adrenaline and preparing to get out of danger. Insecurely attached girls, though, had a "tend and befriend" reaction; they, too, were very anxious, but they did not go away from danger, they went toward it. There is a very important consequence of this: while well-loved children are attracted to peaceful, caring, and warm friends and partners, girls with "tend and befriend" patterns will feel most comfortable around angry/depressed people, who unconsciously remind them of mom. These girls will have a strong belief system that it's their job to choose someone with mood swings or violent tendencies and try to fix them. I don't have to spell out what a problem this can become.

"Tend and befriend" skills have their advantages. In the workplace, women managers are far more likely to sidestep a potential conflict, see someone's aggression as just anxiety, and empathically listen to all sides of a problem. It's a brilliant skill that can bring about world peace as well as happy families. We badly need more of this, and for men to learn it, too; but it has to be a conscious choice, not a compulsion—if it's an unconscious pattern in intimate relationships, it can lead to harm.

If you have a daughter who is always a peacemaker, do affirm and value that, but make sure she can also mobilize some anger when needed, can stand up for herself, and doesn't get used by her friends. If you notice your daughter being too much like this, encourage her to ask, "What do I want for myself?" and be just a little more assertive.

Girls and Sports

Sports are good for girls. Taking part in sports is social, it's physical, it builds confidence, and it allows them to let off steam. Sports are a celebration of our body's capacities, and participating in sports also increases and strengthens those capacities. It's a vital part of healthy girlhood. There is a vast choice now in what you can play and do.

Preschool Age

Under the age of five, the very best sport is to simply play. Go to places where she can run around, have outings to the park, countryside, or the beach with friends or just picnics in the backyard so that there is more encouragement to be active and play games. Organized sports for little ones, like toddler gym or ballet, need to be checked out carefully because structured classes invite comparison and pressure when the girls are way too young. Sometimes these classes are run in a fun way but, in general, informal natural play opportunities are best.

Playgroups are an ideal part of a toddler's week because moms, dads, and kids can all find company and get new skills in a fun environment that is unpressured and inexpensive.

Before Adolescence

Under the age of ten, girls are very open to sports because they have not yet become too self-conscious to enjoy themselves. They are also equal in ability to boys, if not better coordinated. The more different sports

Continued

preadolescent girls take part in, the better, because this helps muscle, bone, and posture development across all their body areas. It's also more fun.

Swimming and climbing are good for upper body development; balance is helped by dance, skating, or court sports (tennis); and team sports involve aerobic exercise and lower body strength. Some girls love the fun and excitement of a team sport and its bonding friendships. But if your daughter really doesn't like team sports, there are lots more individual ones she could try, such as track, or creative options like dance, yoga, or gymnastics that can still give her joy in her body.

By getting some skill in lots of sports, your daughter has the most choice of enjoyable recreation being available when she is a student or young adult. Fun is the aim—watch out for coaches who are anxious or performance driven and who pass this pressure on to the kids. Pressure leads to injuries, because children are forced to move out of their natural grace and pleasure in moving about and strain themselves. Choose sports and coaches who are warm and see the sport as something for the kids, not the other way round. At this age, you want her to enjoy what she does, that way she will want to keep doing it when she is older.

In Adolescence

From ten upward, there are challenges getting some girls to play sports. It helps if the foundations have been laid by lots of interest (perhaps especially from dads) in the earlier years, but still even very sporting girls suddenly don't want to play and won't say why. Often it's about feeling self-conscious—we have made girls so uptight about looking perfect, and in sports, they are more aware of the differences between body shapes and sizes, and there is an uncoordinated phase around the age of thirteen when arms and legs don't seem to do what they want due to brain reorganization.

Worst of all, many girls diet at this age. This is the worst possible time for them to do this because their increased growth rate through adolescence means there's a huge need for calcium (at least 1200 milligrams a day) and energy, as well as vitamins and other minerals, especially iron for menstruating girls. Exercising her body builds the bone strength that she will depend on sixty years later when osteoporosis threatens. Bones grow like at no other time if you use them at this age.

So this is the time to help your daughter find one or two sports that she really enjoys. Remove all obstacles to her playing them, and perhaps get involved as an adult in the transport or coaching so that you can be with her and also support her friends in that sport, because this is an age at which kids appreciate more than just Mom and Dad to talk to and learn from.

The opposite risk—obsessive overemphasis on a sport—is also there, because girls in their teens are capable of losing all sense of perspective. Be sure to check that your superathletic daughter has days off, doesn't train to her detriment, and still eats well and in a relaxed way. Be physical for fun—go to the beach or play volleyball in the backyard and don't let it all be about competition. Some years ago there was an Australian Senate inquiry into abusive training levels in the national gymnastic team—girls were having delayed puberty and were not menstruating until their twenties because of the huge stress put on their bodies through training when they were still so young. This would likely have permanent and damaging effects. It's all about balance!

If your daughter just doesn't like sports, look for activities like dancing, hiking, boogie boarding, kayaking, or fishing, which are individual and noncompetitive but still take joy in movement and being in the physical world. It can be hard if she is shy or just would rather be playing video games, but don't give up trying to find ways she can find joy in her body.

Keep sports fun, sociable, and without too much pressure to win. Make sure the adult mentors are healthy and balanced people, and if they are not, change to a different team or a different sport. Get involved, too, so that you can get to know and care about her friends, who perhaps won't all have parents who are so good-hearted.

What Happens In Puberty?

Puberty in girls starts on average at about age ten, but it's incredibly variable—it can be any time between ages eight and sixteen! It's important to prepare your daughter for this phase so she has a positive attitude and feels informed and grown up about it.

BREASTS

The first sign of puberty for most girls is breast budding. Usually this becomes apparent as a firm tender lump under the nipple of one or both breasts. Within six months, this is usually on both sides and spreading wider than the areola (the dark area around the nipple). After another twelve months, the breast usually has grown to something like its mature size and shape.

But breast development is incredibly variable, and it's important to explain this to your girl. Being the first in your class to have breasts can cause embarrassment, and breasts arriving a bit late may worry some girls, especially in our sexualized environment when such things are made into a bigger deal than they should be.

PUBIC HAIR

Within a couple of months of breast changes beginning, pubic hair starts to grow, at first around the labia (lips) of the vagina and later spreading up to the mound around her lower abdomen. In about 15 percent of girls, though, pubic hair starts growing before breasts start to bud. Everyone is different.

MENSTRUATION

Usually about two years after the start of breast budding, or around age twelve in most girls, the first menstrual bleeding happens. This is so variable, though, that you should tell your daughter about it long before you suspect it might happen, just to be on the safe side. Remember, some girls can start their periods as early as age eight. (We still hear of girls finding blood on their panties and not knowing what is wrong, being terrified that they have done something wrong, or being deeply embarrassed because nobody prepared them.)

You can tell her about pads and tampons; she may already be familiar with you talking about periods and managing them, and if you have a positive attitude that really helps. Rather than seeing menstruation as just a nuisance, focus on the big picture that this is a great sign of growing up and being able to one day have babies if she chooses. Remind her that having her periods shouldn't stop her from doing almost anything she wants. Be happy for her, and she will catch that spirit. Let her carry a slim pad in her purse or bag in case she needs it, and let her know that she can also ask the nurse at school in an emergency.

In the first few years, periods are not regular. They can come at any time. Ovulation (where an egg is released and she can get pregnant) doesn't always happen with early periods; it may take several years before a girl ovulates on *every* cycle, but you can't rely on that. You, and she, need to know that pregnancy is now a possibility.

HIPS

Girls will get more chubby about eighteen months before puberty begins—usually around age eight or nine. This is often the first sign of puberty being on its way. As the estrogen levels in her body rise, her hips and pelvis will widen (to make it easier for babies to be born). She will often have a growth spurt and become much taller, too, at this time, becoming close to her adult final height.

OTHER STUFF

Vaginas clean themselves, and sometimes a whitish secretion comes from a girl's vagina once puberty has begun. Tell your daughter about this, too, and that it's healthy and normal.

Skin gets a lot oilier in puberty, which can be a bit of a pain. Pimples and acne are more common, and also girls sweat much more. Help your daughter find natural and healthy ways to manage this—stay away from chemicals or harsh treatments, if you can.

CELEBRATE

Don't make puberty sound like a big negative; it's really important to convey the excitement and amazement of being a woman. Some people have a special mother, aunties, grandmas, and daughter grown-up dinner, or go camping together or to a nice hotel. Some people devise rituals or sharing times for their daughters with the women who love them. Celebrate. This is a time for honoring and appreciating your daughter's success in growing up well.

In a Nutshell

* Friends are really important to girls.
* Between five and ten social skills are being learned big time.
* There are seven key skills: enjoying the company of others, sharing, empathy, controlling aggression, apologizing, reading emotions, and knowing whom to trust. She will need help to learn these.
* She will learn by copying you, too.
* Each of the four emotions (anger, fear, sorrow, and joy) have a purpose to guide her.
* "Tend and befriend" is a useful skill, but it can get out of control. Sometimes you need "fight or flight."
* Sports can be great, especially if you can find the right one for your girl.
* Understand about puberty and prepare your daughter well in advance—by about the age of eight!

CHAPTER FIVE

Finding Her Soul
(Ten to Fourteen Years)

Often by late elementary school girls can seem very grown up, sensible, and mature.

Parents heave a sigh of relief and wonder if that job is done. Of course, as everyone knows, this is just the lull before the storm! Soon the hormonal rockets fire up, and the next adventure begins. The timing of puberty varies greatly, but whenever it comes, it has a profound effect. Up until now, most girls have been unself-conscious, rambunctious kids who live happily for today. They ride, swim, make noise, play sports, get involved in creative activities, and generally breeze through life. Their confidence and can-do attitude makes them a joy to be around.

Puberty doesn't necessarily change this, but it adds a new "inwardness" to a girl's nature. She senses adulthood is coming toward her and, prompted by those unmistakable signals, she can't help but start to think about the kind of woman she is to become. There is excitement, as well as fear, and even sadness at the loss of childhood freedom and simplicity. This often makes her more reflective and somewhat more private. Observant dads and moms will notice this distinct change of "season" in their daughter. A girl at this age starts to ask herself, "Who am I?" "What do I want?" "What is my life really about?" Her answers to these questions will guide her choices through the next decade of her life.

Take every chance she gives you, on car trips, while doing tasks together, or as you sit with her in her room at bedtime, to listen to what she says and to ask her about her thoughts about her life and her world. You will find you start to share more about your own life, your teen experiences, your beliefs and ideas, and that she is now more ready to listen. Suddenly you are not so distant in age.

Preparation Begins in Earnest

The years from ten to fourteen are far more important than most people realize—they are not something to skip over. This is a time of intense preparation. We have to help girls to stay in this place and not to rush into premature attempts at being grown up, for which they are far from ready. If you take nothing else from this chapter, or even this whole book, please take this: girls from ten to fourteen years old need more, not less, of our time, interest, and *availability*. This is when we ramp up our teaching, explaining, coaching, inquiring, and when we involve her in more demanding activity, preparing her to be the amazing woman she can become. But we don't push her out there alone yet, or let the world grab her with its pressures to conform, compete, be sexual, or please boys in order to feel okay. She is preparing for womanhood, but that preparation is a stage all of its own.

Spark

Between the ages of ten and fourteen, a girl's job is to get her roots down deep into who she is. There are many ways to do this. The first, and easiest, is called "spark."

Dr. Peter Benson, who died tragically young in 2011, was the founder of the Search Institute in the US and one of the world's leading experts on adolescence. Peter spent the final years of his life campaigning for one single idea that he felt could transform the quality of both home and school life for young people—the idea that we all have a "spark."

When parents are asked what are their aspirations for their daughters they hardly ever say things like "to make our nation more internationally competitive" or "to get high scores on the SATs during senior year." Parents say, "I want her to love life," or "I want her to be kind and compassionate," or "I want her to find her passion in life and follow it." We love our kids, and so our goals for them are founded in that: we want them to find deep satisfaction in their hearts.

The question is, how? Peter Benson discovered something that seems so simple, but it is a complete game-changer. He discovered that children and young teenagers almost always have something inside them—an interest, enthusiasm, talent, or concern—which, if it is supported, gives them incredible joy, motivation, and direction. That thing is their *spark*.

His studies found the following remarkable facts:

* Asked the question, "What activity gives you the most joy, makes you feel most alive, gives you a sense of purpose and excitement?" 100 percent of children understood the idea.

* About 65 percent of all kids could tell you at least one activity that filled those criteria for them. They knew what their spark was.

* Another 20 percent, when prompted by an adult who knew them, could also find their spark (they were just too shy to say so straight out).

* Of these children, 10 percent had more than one thing that sparked them. Lucky kids!

Benson loved to quote the ancient philosopher Plutarch, who said, "The young are not vessels to be filled, they are fires to be lit." Those teachers who understand this are the ones who are loved by kids and appreciated by parents.

HOW ABOUT YOUR DAUGHTER?

Does your daughter have a spark? Do you know what it is? Is her spark alight, or is it going out? What would it take to see it really burning bright?

The key to your daughter finding herself and beginning to really blossom as a person, at age ten to fourteen (or younger), might be as simple as asking her, "What do you really love to do?" and "How can I help you to do that?" "What are the obstacles to doing it that I can help you overcome?" "Who else do we need to get on board (at school or in the community) to be able to do that?"

To help parents with this spark chasing, Benson separated sparks into three kinds:

* A skill or talent—for instance, to draw, write, be athletic, dance, or make music. Your child is just naturally good at this, and she enjoys doing it greatly.

* A commitment—for example to protect the natural world, or to work for social justice. It's the power of their caring that powers them along.

* A quality of character—a part of their personality, such as empathy—being the one who others go to talk to. Or courage—being the one who speaks up or takes the lead to get something fixed. (If something is happening, you can bet it will be your child out at the front!)

Benson believes our job is to confirm and strengthen our child's spark—to blow on it and help it ignite. "If you discover a kid's spark, tell it back to them, tell them you see and hear it, thank them for possessing it. In almost all cases, it's good, beautiful, and useful to the world." Of course, identifying her spark is just the beginning of some serious work for you as her parent to enable it to start to burn. But what could be more worthwhile?

NOT ALL SPARKS ARE KEPT ALIVE

It's here that Benson points out a tragic thing, and it was this that became his life's mission. Only about a quarter of the young people he studied were truly thriving in their lives—happy, engaged, and with a strong sense of where they were going. He believed this was in most cases because the adults in their lives had not kept those kids' sparks alive, or even found out what they were.

He believed that there are *three critical things* that are required in a young girl if her spark is to burn brightly.

1. There must be an adult *in her family* who gets behind her.

2. She also needs an adult *outside* the family—at school or in the community—who recognizes and helps her.

3. There has to be the *opportunity* to encourage her spark and carry out whatever it needs to be lit.

How many of us as adults had an interest that our parents couldn't be bothered to support? Or perhaps our parents were positive, but nobody at school cared, or there just wasn't a way in the community we lived in to follow that interest. How many millions of sparks just went out for lack of those ingredients? Surely we can do it differently.

WHY IT MATTERS

Why bother? What does it really matter? Peter Benson's research indicates that this discovery of an enthusiasm (and the support to follow it) affects some very important benchmarks. Children with sparks do better at school; they are happier and more confident, they engage better with adults, they get into less trouble with their health and well-being, or with the law or school. (We shouldn't really need these other reasons to want our kids to be happy, but there they are.)

Your daughter's spark may change through life. We as adults know that sometimes we move on from one thing to another, but we take with us the sense of focus, application, self-belief, and creativity. But equally often, these sparks give us pleasure for life. A spark may become our career or it may not, but it is definitely at the heart of who we are. Your spark is your way of being in the world— artist, creator, writer, athlete, leader, caregiver, inventor, mystic, activist—this is your deep self, and that fire will keep you alive and sparking until the end of your days.

A Different Group of Friends

There is another reason why an activity or interest enriches or strengthens a girl. It provides her with an alternative *reference group* that may give her a much larger and more positive view of herself.

Often girls are trapped with only one friendship group—the accidental assemblage of same-age girls they meet at school. Apart from home (which also has its ups and downs), they have no other view of themselves. A girl can easily find her spirits sinking dangerously low because her peer group is too negative or destructive, but an interest group may be much more her kind of people. Also there may be mixed ages with all the benefits this brings. Interesting and wise old men, feisty and eccentric women, friends from other schools or suburbs who are much more on her maturity level or share her interests. This gives her a different mirror in which she can see herself.

There are astonishing ranges of interests available to young girls, from Latin dance to rock climbing, quilting to scuba diving. There are hundreds of ways in which they can volunteer and be useful. Think outside the box of packaged activities that girls are supposed to do, and instead consider interests that people in the adult world pursue with passion. Don't merely crowd her life with multiple classes or activities after school; instead help her to search for just that kind of group where she feels really at home, and support her in letting that blossom.

A Place to Make and Do

If I could organize it, every girl would have a place to make and do—a kind of workshop/craft room or corner of the house peacefully away from TV sounds or smaller children, where messes could be left and projects take shape among endless materials, paints, tools, and so on. "Making"—the creation of beautiful things—has emerged in recent years as a rediscovered expression of individuality, a way to be serene and an answer to the consumer madness in which girls express themselves merely by what they buy. Sculpture, painting, pottery, self-created fashion, art, and craft of any kind seem to have a strengthening and healing effect on both boys and girls. Having a "women's space" in the house that is sacrosanct and their own, just as men have their "man caves" or workshops, would be ideal.

Since few of us have houses that allow dedicated space, another option is just a desk or a corner that is her own place—not for schoolwork but for a freely chosen creativity.

Some communities around the world have begun to set up girls' and women's spaces—this might just be a weekly event in a borrowed room or hall where older women make teenage girls welcome in circles of creativity and earthy talk, and girls who are sometimes bordering on becoming street kids find a haven and a shoulder to lean on.

Actions You Can Take

Knowing your child's spark is a priority of a parent of a young teenager. It will help if you can remember your own spark history. What did you love to do as a child? Did it stay the same or change? Did your spark go out? What sparks your life now?

Discussing a child's spark should be part of every parent–teacher meeting. Schools should know the children's sparks and should help you find ways to encourage them.

Community groups and recreation departments should conduct surveys of the sparks that local children have and plan to provide those facilities and services to make sure they are encouraged.

All That You Have Is Your Soul

When my wife was a nurse in training in the 1970s, aged just seventeen, sometimes a patient would die. Shaaron would fetch the matron of the small country hospital, who would come into the room and do a rather strange thing—she would open the window just a crack. This was to let that person's soul leave. This is not what I mean here by soul (though I am not making fun of that idea, and perhaps they are related). When Tracey Chapman sang "All That You Have Is Your Soul," she was talking about the deep-down essence of a person— who they really are, and what matters most to them. Soul is a hard thing to express in words, but everyone knows when a person has it. Some quite young people have soul, though it tends to come with experience, especially hard experience. Some folks clearly have none at all. They are selfish, shallow, anxious, and grasping. They blow about in the slightest breeze. A person with soul is like a tree with deep roots, steady in the gale.

Watch a ten-year-old girl closely, and you will see her starting to grow deeper roots. She dreams dreams that are her own private and fragile longings, which are not for sharing with other people. She asks big questions, and she watches the adults around her for clues as to how to live.

Soul is a place inside you where you know what's right and what's wrong. While everybody has this place inside them, not everybody has traveled there. It needs people around us to gently, sincerely, nudge us to find it. Sometimes poetry helps, or a movie. or a song. When her favorite auntie takes a girl out and in a quiet moment asks, "What do you really want to do with your life?" it invites a girl into her soul. Nobody gives you soul, although they can show you theirs.

Soul means knowing yourself. If you break your own rules, nobody else will know, but you will hate yourself until you put things right. Soul is creative, it draws you to unique and special pathways, activities, means of expressing yourself. Soul is the real you. You can pretend to be someone else—some people do that all their lives. Many women through history have hidden their real selves away and had a kind of suffocation of the spirit as a result. When you are being true to yourself, it feels right, even if nobody around you even *begins* to understand.

Daughters need this quality, at the ordinary everyday level as well as the lifetime level—when they fight with friends, or decide what to do or where to go, when a friend is getting drunk and wants them to be drunk, too, or some boys ask them to pile into a car late at night, or her friends are being horrible to another girl at school. When she sees that her body in the mirror is a different shape than the air-brushed bodies in the magazines, her soul whispers to her: "I am me, and I am beautiful as I am."

When she chooses what to study, who to be friends with, what career to follow, who to date or marry, the voice of her soul is the one she should listen to.

Learning from Anne Frank

In 1945, a young girl's diary came to light, written in very unusual circumstances. Anne Frank is perhaps the most famous teenage girl in history. She wrote such a lucid and poignant account of her inner world that it has become a classic book. What parent hasn't wished they could see into the heart of their fourteen-year-old girl?

Anne Frank was thirteen, in 1938 when her family went into hiding from the Nazis, in German-occupied Holland. Along with her parents and an older sister, Anne was kept safe in the attic of an old factory by her father's loyal employees and stayed there undetected for almost two years. They were joined by several others during that time, including a teenage boy, Peter, with whom Anne eventually enjoyed a tender teenage romance. Conditions were awful, she had to share her room with an older man who was moody and selfish, they were hungry, and the fear was constant. They knew from a small radio what was happening to Jewish people across Europe and would happen to them, too, if they were found.

As Anne moved through the experience of adolescence, she recorded everything. She was not especially close to her mother— mothers in those days were not always as warm as most are today—and she placed more trust in her father, who was kind and affectionate although somewhat mystified by his daughter. "I model myself on Father, and there's no one in the world I love more," she declared, but she was not really happy with his response to her.

"He doesn't realize that he treats Margot differently from me. Margot just happens to be the cleverest, the kindest, the prettiest and the best. But I have a right to be taken seriously too. I've always been the clown and mischief-maker of the family; I've always had to pay double for my sins, once with scolding and then again with my own sense of despair. I'm no longer satisfied with the meaningless affection or the supposedly serious talks. I long for something from Father that he's incapable of giving. I'm not jealous of Margot; I never have been. It's just that I'd like to feel that Father really loves me, not because I'm his child, but because I'm me, Anne."

Of her mother, Anne was harsher.

"She's not a mother to me—I have to mother myself. I've cut myself adrift from them. I'm charting my own course. I have no choice because I can picture what a mother and wife should be and can't seem to find anything of the sort in the woman I'm supposed to call 'Mother.'"

This wasn't just a bad day; twelve months later, the picture is still the same:

"Despite all my theories and efforts I miss—every day and every hour—having a mother who understands me."

For a midteenager, Anne was remarkably wise and self-aware.

"The best remedy for those who are frightened, lonely or unhappy is to go outside, somewhere they can be alone, alone with the sky, nature and God. For then and only then can you feel that everything is as it should be and that God wants people to be happy amid nature's beauty and simplicity. I firmly believe nature can bring comfort to all who suffer."

In our girl stages, in terms of finding her soul, Anne Frank is right on track.

She gives an especially strong clue to parents about the need to acknowledge their daughters as unique and different and hear out their stories.

"I didn't want to hear about "typical adolescent problems" or "other girls" or "you'll grow out of it." I didn't want to be treated as all-the-other-girls but as Anne-in-her-own right."

She writes about her longings for love; she and Peter, the only boy in her confined universe, sit for hours each day holding each other close, drinking in the sweetness of someone else's caring, but she also comes to see that he is not her future match (they simply don't have enough in common), and so it goes no further.

Anne was also a natural feminist.

"Men presumably dominated women from the very beginning because of their greater physical strength . . . until recently women silently went along with this, which was stupid, since the longer it's kept up, the more deeply entrenched it becomes. Fortunately, education, work and progress have opened women's eyes. Women should be respected as well! What I condemn are our system of values and the men who don't acknowledge how great, difficult, but ultimately beautiful women's share in society is."

And she is strong.

"I have a great deal of self-knowledge. In everything I do I can watch myself as if I were a stranger. I can stand across from the everyday Anne and without being biased or making excuses watch what she's doing, both good and bad. In addition, I face life with an extraordinary amount of courage. I feel so strong and capable of bearing burdens, so young and free!"

Then one day in August 1944, they are discovered. A sudden crashing in of doors, an arrest, and a three-day journey in a cattle train to Auschwitz. On arrival, her hair is shaved off and a number tattooed on her body. The last sighting of Anne describes her standing by a barbed-wire fence, "bald, emaciated, shivering." She died just days later. She was only fifteen.

The Dutch people bravely hid and saved 20,000 Jewish people. Of the 100,000 Dutch Jews captured by the Nazis, only 5,000 survived.

Anne's diary became one of the best-known books in the world. It was read by Nelson Mandela in prison, and he said it gave him great heart.

What Works for Developing Soul?

One way in which you can help your daughter develop soul is by finding the right people to bring into her life. Many people can be role models for your daughter and can show her how to be a strong, deep woman. These women include teachers both at school and in the special interests she may have, such as music, art, or yoga, or perhaps some special sports coaches; young women in their twenties or thirties who help on camps and retreats; old people who love having girls at their house, including aunts or grandmothers who have lived rich and interesting lives. All have their own *interiority* (a quiet strength inside themselves) and this automatically draws out the same in girls.

Choose these people on a simple criteria: that your own soul is drawn to them. They seem at peace, warm-hearted as opposed to merely being "nice," and are gutsy and eccentric rather than bland and ordinary. Choose women who are interested in your daughter as an individual and who see something special in her. It has to be a mutual enjoyment. (At this age, the mentor role is safer when it's same-sex, but there may be wonderful exceptions and some women report about having had great male role models, too.)

Some activities build soul, while others harm it. Avoid what is intensely competitive or performance-oriented unless your daughter has a real love for these activities and can't be stopped! Creative activity done for its own sake builds your daughter's soul; it can be as varied as sculpture, working on motorcycles, or as advanced as writing her own fantasy novel. All these things draw a girl into a sense of peace and reflection, as she is present in doing them.

Books are important as both inspiration and refuge. When we read, we journey inward—we can't help doing so, because the printed word triggers our own minds to fill in the gaps in a way that a movie can't. And we are taken into other lives, places, and times in a way that expands our own sense of what is possible. Many people have had their lives changed by a single book. Adolescents hunger for spirit food, and books often provide this.

Time in nature is something that is often denied to girls because of safety fears. Wandering in woodlands near one's home (the joy of boys since time began) is seen as too risky. But do what you can to provide opportunities for her to be in wild and beautiful places (family holidays are a great way to do this), where she can surf, swim, ride, hike, or sail. Do some of these things with her, too, because she needs to see you away from your normal, humdrum self.

Keep Calm and Keep on Loving

Girls get onto an emotional roller coaster when they hit their teens, and these years can be trying for their parents as they pick their way through the minefield, hoping not to trigger any explosions!

The early-teens phase seems to go in two leaps. First, around thirteen (sometimes a bit younger), girls seem to become mentally unstuck. The reason is that the rapid rewiring of the prefrontal cortex (which is described on page 25) mostly begins at thirteen. The effect is that she becomes very babylike, disorganized, and helpless. It can be exasperating, but she is just revisiting babyhood. Keep a close watch on her and enjoy the fact that she at least loves being close, cuddling, and hanging out with you. At fourteen, another phase completely kicks in.

Fourteen can be a cranky stage. The teenager has a job to do—to start getting free of her parents. She has been, all being well, embedded in her family and defined by them, and her whole world is part of the family's network. Now that has to change, or she will never make it on her own. It's important not to see this as a rejection process—it isn't based on not liking you. A girl might adore her parents and everything they stand for, but something deep inside her knows that she can't grow from inside her parents' world; she has to get out and be herself. It can lead to all kinds of trying on of identities, such as taking on Goth, punk, or grunge appearances to escape a neat and respectable family. Sometimes parents get huffy about this rebellion and back off. But it's not a time for abandoning your daughter. She has to fight, argue, cajole, reason, and make a case with someone; it's either you, or the police, or her teachers. Better that it's you.

Of course, much of the time she will be just fine, but when she does seem difficult or impossible, don't panic. Deal with it, listen, make your case, grant her some leeway if she argues well, or agree to disagree. She is learning to be her own person, even though she isn't sure what that is yet. It's tough on parents. The old bottom lines about safety and keeping her side of the bargain still count, but get your friendship needs met somewhere else, because your daughter won't want (always) to be your friend at this age.

Fifteen is usually easier; and by sixteen, most girls have mellowed a great deal. Once she is more sure of herself, she doesn't have to flick you away and she will feel that she can be friends with you again.

Into the Wild

Kym Pitman is an experienced outdoor educator, as well as a noted singer-songwriter, mother, and aunt. She retired from teaching to develop what she has long felt is the ideal way to help young women grow deep roots and be nourished for their lifetime journey as women.

Kym takes adolescent girls on ten-day retreat hikes into the Australian wilderness of the mid–north coast in New South Wales, during which

they dispense with almost all of the props of modern life. The girls leave behind cell phones and MP3 players, makeup and media, watches, mirrors, and worries about what to wear and how to look. There is a period of intense disorientation as these props sink from view, and then the loveliness and richness of the rainforest valleys begins to replace them. The scent of silky oak blossom, the birdlife, the caress of cool river water on tired feet, the view overhead in the inky night of the "million-star hotel."

Under Kym's guidance, these young women start to find themselves, not as separate beings, but part of a web that is both harsh and soft, dangerous and lovely, depending on their skill, strength, and judgment.

The experience is a thousand miles from the ordeals that some high-fee-charging schools put their adolescents through in the name of rites of passage, which valorize the athletic and the naturally strong and victimize the gentler or less physically endowed. Some of these seem to be barely concealed sadism, an attempt to squash adolescent energies as much as liberate them. Other school programs half-grasp the importance of learning self-reliance but fail to provide a true connection with nature—just blistered feet and scratched faces and the sense of having fought through, rather than truly merged with, the wild.

Kym is gentle and extremely capable at the same time, and it's a combination that fascinates her young charges. She role-models respect: for oneself, each other, and the deep ecology of river and earth, animal and bird, universe and individual. Fireside talking, journaling exercises, and teaching on the trail begin to open the girls to seeing the world directly as it is—complex and interconnected to their own bodies, with rhythms they can learn from and peace they can rest in.

A climactic point is reached when the girls spend a day in silence and sleep at a distance from each other to experience being alive in the absolute unmediated wild. Their accounts of this period are revealing:

"I don't want to describe it all because I don't want to take away from the experience, and no words could do it justice."

"Yesterday was one of the most beautiful days of my life."

"I close my eyes and breathe in the day. There are no words for what I feel."

"The feeling of green surrounds me, enters me, fulfills me, and talks to me in ways other than speech. I think it speaks in a dialect which is emotion of some sort—love."

"All my senses are alert. The silence is addictive. I wish it would not stop. It makes me feel so peaceful, yet I am joyous all along. Even though it is silent, I feel much more connected to the wildlife all around me and the plants. The feeling I am getting is so very hard to explain. It's almost like I feel I am part of the land. I feel threaded."

Should Girls Have Privacy from Their Moms?

A good guide to privacy, which you can explain to your daughter, is if her door is open you can knock and go in. If it's closed, you will knock, then wait for her to say "come in" before you enter. That's because it's great for her to feel she has some private space and has control over it. When you do go into her room, don't snoop or poke about; nobody likes that. Of course, you can still say, "This room needs tidying" and "Would you like some help?" But just the courtesy of asking her permission gives her a feeling of being respected.

Privacy is a privilege, though, and if she has been doing something secretive or strange (see eating disorders, page 150, or having problems with drinking or drugs, page 155) then you may opt to let her know that you will keep an eye out in her room. Safety takes precedence over privacy, but forewarn her all the same. For complicated reasons, it's best if only Mom does this. Your daughter can be angry at Mom, but she would be outraged if Dad were to invade her space. If all is fine, though, privacy is a great thing that we all like to have.

Aunties

At the start of this book, we pinpointed a huge mental health decline among girls. We asked how could this be—what is going wrong? One possibility is that we have *forgotten how to do aunty-ing*.

I often ask audiences, "Who had an auntie who made a big difference in your life?" About a third of all women put their hands up. The older they are, the higher the number. Today aunties have progressively disappeared from the lives of girls.

By Auntie with a capital A, I am referring to real aunts (sisters of her dad or mom), plus adult friends of her mother or family who take a personal interest in her well-being. (Grandmothers have a slightly different role, as an anchor more than as a role model—their age puts them beyond a girl's imagination!) Every girl needs at least one special Auntie.

As an adult reading this, think of any nieces (or for men, nephews) you may have. Consider if you could be a more-involved Auntie to them. Auntie-ing could mean:

1. Having her over to your house for meals or sometimes to stay. This can be a great respite from home and a chance for real conversations about how she is getting on. If you sense that she is relaxed and likes it, do it every few months. As she begins to feel comfortable with you, when she has crises or deep concerns, she is likely to share them with you and seek your advice.

2. Taking her for a regular coffee or shopping trip to town and talking to her like she is a thoughtful adult. Asking about her life, her dreams, her challenges. Doing it not with a sense of problem seeking, but of taking the long view, finding out her perspective. Just do a lot of listening.

3. Remembering her birthday, going to her school concerts or sports games.

Continued

4. Offering help with practical or financial challenges that she may have in pursuing her dreams. Being sensitive to her mother and father, augmenting just a little the team she has rooting for her:

"My auntie paid for my piano lessons."

"She took me into the city every school holiday. We had afternoon teas and pretended we were ladies!"

"When my brother died in a car crash, I went and lived at her house for three months. My parents were just too devastated to function. It was a relief to be somewhere more normal, though I went home at weekends. It was lifesaving for everyone."

"My Auntie knew about my boyfriend and the problems we had. I just couldn't tell Mom."

"My Auntie was younger than my mom by about six years, she just understood better. She taught me about menstruation and periods. You could ask her about anything."

"I would go to my Auntie's, and we would make mosaics together. I just loved doing it with her."

As well as deeply listening, Aunties also talk sense to girls; they know about boys and men and are straight talkers:

"Sure, he's good-looking. But he's really dull. You'd be bored after ten minutes."

"That boy is a player. I wouldn't trust a word he says. He needs ten years to grow up."

"It's not you he loves, sugar, it's your boobs."

Aunties also aren't afraid to criticize you. "You're really just scared of being rejected" or "I think that's wrong—you need to go and tell your Mom you're sorry."

"You could do that, but you'd be copping out. You are capable of more than that."

The job of being an Auntie or an Uncle is much more important than we have realized, but you have to want to play the part, or see the need and step up. You can't do it on a whim, because a young person will be heartbroken if you let her down. It has to be for the long haul—especially through the difficult passage of adolescence. If you feel an affinity with your niece, try it. It will be mutually enriching; she will give you a sense of freshness and clarity in return. Aunties are as ancient as the stones, and we are wired to need them.

Early Puberty, Chemicals, and Your Girl

Many people have been getting alarmed about girls starting puberty sooner, and with good reason. When a girl of eight develops breasts, it's bound to cause her some confusion and bring undue attention. Is there an epidemic of early puberty? What's causing it? And what can we do to prevent it from happening to our daughters?

Puberty is driven by hormones, and for the last hundred years our wonderful industrial system has been making chemicals that mimic those hormones, both on purpose and by accident. Today hormone mimics and hormone disruptors like bisphenol A (BPA) and pthalates occur in products we use every day and in agricultural chemicals that show up in our water and food.

We've known about this for forty years. In Italy in 1977, contaminated beef and poultry caused hundreds of boys and girls at a school near Milan to begin growing breasts. Contaminated feed for cattle in Michigan in 1973 affected both milk and beef from those cows, and pregnant mothers who consumed these gave birth to daughters who experienced significantly earlier puberty. And in 2005, a brother and sister aged three and four began growing pubic hair because their dad had been using testosterone cream bought on the Internet and normal daily contact with his kids was enough to rub it off on them. Silly man.

Hormones are not like ordinary chemicals—they operate in infinitesimally small doses. A single molecule of hormone is enough to create a reaction, so to talk of safe levels is scientific nonsense. If hormones are there, they are almost certainly affecting you.

Puberty changes are one effect, but cancer, diabetes, cardiac problems, even behavioral and mental health problems, have also been linked to these chemicals. A study at the Harvard School of Public Health found that the exposure of *pregnant moms* to BPA correlated with toddlers' behavior problems, aggressiveness, hyperactivity and raised levels of depression. And importantly, *it was only the girl children that were affected*, indicating that it really was a female hormone being disrupted, probably in their brains while they were in the womb.

The US Department of Health and Human Services looked at hundreds of research studies into the plastics additive BPA and found "undisputed evidence" that it affects mammary glands. It's fairly safe to say, these chemicals are not good for you or your girl. So what are we to do?

What Can You Do?

Let's start with the easy ones. Many people have heard that BPA is in polycarbonate water bottles (check for the recycling number 7 on the bottom) and, until recently, in *baby bottles*. And yes, it does leach out—students in one study who used these bottles had a 69 percent increase in their levels *after just one week!*

Worse news is that BPA is also found in the liners of cans which are used for vegetables and soups. This is a much greater source than drink bottles because of the longer exposure that food has to the lining, during which it will interact with it. Canned tomato soup, which is slightly acid, is a good one to avoid right away. Canned soft drinks and alcoholic drinks also leach BPA into their contents. If you use baby formula, the powder is a lot safer than liquids. Plastic cling wraps on foods should be avoided, unless you can find one that is BPA-free—and *never* heat them or microwave them.

Finally, BPA is also present on the thermal paper used for supermarket receipts and airline boarding passes, although safe alternatives do exist. For people who work on supermarket checkouts, this is of special concern.

Hormone mimics are also present in agricultural sprays, so eating organic is a good idea if you can, and try to buy meat from grass-fed rather than grain-fed animals. (It's also healthier for you and, of course, the cows.)

Some of the recommendations are really hard to carry out and, in fact, require legislative change. What the heck can you or I do about furniture treated with fire retardants? How would we know if a mattress or clothing is chemically treated? (If it smells chemical, *it probably is.* Give it a good airing before having it near you. But not all chemicals smell.)

And finally, cosmetics often have pthalates—nail polish and artificial fragrances are common culprits. (Check out the Campaign for Safe Cosmetics website for details.) Use fragrance-free detergents, cleansers, personal care products, and avoid air fresheners unless their label clearly states "pthalate-free." *Many air fresheners contain phthalates, and, of course, you breathe these in.*

If this makes you feel like living in a cabin in the woods, I don't blame you. It's the job of politicians and regulators to manage these things, but industry lobbies continually to keep us in the dark. In the meantime, a pregnant mom who works on a checkout, uses nail polish, drinks soft drink out of a can, heats canned soup for dinner, and eats grain-fed beef should probably hope for a boy!

What to Do about Premature Puberty

When girls experience premature signs of puberty, such as breast growth, there are a range of reasons.

* Beyond exposure to hormone disruptors, there are syndromes that cause early puberty, such as CPP, or central precocious puberty. These girls might show signs of puberty as young as three to six years old, for example. These conditions can be treated by drugs and managed well.

* Some girls simply do enter puberty very young and always have. It is a small proportion, but still a significant number, and it varies hugely by race. By age seven, 10 percent of white girls, 23 percent of black girls, 15 percent of hispanic girls, and 2 percent of Asian girls have started developing breasts. Specialists do not recommend treating these conditions because they are part of the normal range.

* To say that more girls are entering puberty younger is not strictly true; what is happening is that more and more girls are having breast budding younger, but this is not true puberty— that is, it does not correspond to the other changes. The age of actual menarche (the start of periods) has changed very little over the last forty years and is still a little past the age of twelve. (Though it can be as late as sixteen; so don't worry, there are late bloomers in every group of girls.)

* The research into girls who had early breast development found that in many of these girls, the usual estrogens from the body at puberty (estradiol) were not present. This led to the conclusion that it was estrogen-like chemicals from the environment that were triggering a kind of "false start." Breast growth of this kind did not bring forward the age of first menstruation, and true puberty stayed on its normal track.

* Early breast growth increases the lifetime risk of cancer, and, perhaps more importantly, having breast development at eight or nine brings on social attention that in our sexualized world a girl is far from ready to deal with. It's this latter fact that has caused parents most concern.

There are several other reasons as to why puberty starts sooner:

* Having a lot of body fat. Body fat actually creates estrogen and starts a vicious circle, because estrogen then tells the body to lay down more fat. (See the chapter on weight issues for help with this.) Don't let your daughter start dieting or force her into more exercise; these responses often backfire.

* Having a lot of stress. Girls whose parents divorced between the ages of three and eight, or those who had fathers who were violent, alcohol- or drug-dependent, suicidal, or spent time in prison were more likely to have early puberty.

* Having a stepdad. This is not because stepdads are stressful, but probably because an unrelated male in the home affects girls' hormones in some way we don't understand.

* Being from a developing country or suffering early starvation. Adopted orphans and refugees who have settled in developed countries as young children often show early puberty. Our best explanation for this is that the body decides life is tough, better get on with it.

So what can you do if your daughter starts puberty really young, say at age seven or eight? We can't change the fact that our daughters start puberty early, but we can change how we deal with it. We can encourage them to be active and enjoy their bodies. We can treat them as the age they are and not be influenced by the way they look. We can stand up to a world that markets bras (even push-up bras!) for six-year-olds and puts them in beauty pageants with makeup and coy moves. We can keep their childhood happy and relaxed by not buying into competiveness, having family meals together, reading books together, and letting them be young. Early puberty can be disconcerting, but it's not a recipe for disaster. We can manage it and keep their lives on track.

If Your Daughter Is a Lesbian

There has been enormous progress in the last few years in accepting and understanding young people who are same-sex attracted. There are politicians, rock stars, athletes, actors, teachers, pastors, and broadcasters who are happily and publicly gay and almost nobody blinks an eye.

On the other hand, there are still people who regard lesbian, gay, bisexual, or transgender (LGBT*) orientation as some kind of evil choice or an illness that needs a cure. This viewpoint is, fortunately, decreasing,

* LGBT (Lesbian, Gay, Bisexual, Transgender) is the now commonly accepted term for people who don't fit the neat categories of "straight" heterosexuality. Gay is sometimes used as shorthand for all categories, but most people use "lesbian" as the simplest way to denote girls who are primarily attracted to other girls. Transgender girls—who feel intrinsically like boys and may or may not actually have treatment to become more physically male—are another category that we haven't addressed in this book. The issues for parents remain the same in terms of acceptance and support for her in discovering who she really is.

Continued

perhaps as people simply get to know the facts and to know gay people in person.

For a parent, this growing acceptance is helpful, but it still has a far way to go. Being a parent of a same-sex-attracted daughter is still a road that takes some courage to walk.

The Facts

Society's default assumption is that everyone is straight. Even for the young person concerned, the discovery that she is same-sex attracted may come as something of a shock. Then there is the question of how to let others know—especially Mom and Dad. A young person may be terrified that her parents won't accept her, or will react badly to the news. Recognizing that you are same-sex attracted usually happens in the early teens, which is a hard-enough time already for fitting in and believing in yourself. This situation needs sensitivity and help from all around your child.

Whatever your child's sexual orientation turns out to be, it helps if all through her growing up that *your language* about gay and lesbian people is understanding and not derogatory, and you have taken the trouble to read about or gotten to know a little of the LGBT experience. A Dad (or Mom) who mocks or puts down gay people is not going to invite openness in their own kids.

The process of acknowledging, first in oneself, then to one's parents and then one's wider circle of friends and family, is a series of decisions a young person has to think about. Most gay adults will tell you that "coming out"—letting the world know by degrees that you are not quite what they think you are—is a long journey. If your daughter discovers she is LGBT, she is the only one who can decide about whom she tells, and when. Some young people are totally comfortable, free, and proud about their sexual orientation, others not at all so, and this may depend on the attitudes of those around them.

There is an inner journey for parents, too. Long before we become parents, even when we are still children ourselves, we dream of the children we will have. Parenthood is nurtured and powered by thoughts of the future. Our dreams run out ahead of us, and weddings and grandchildren often feature in these fantasies!

The power of these dreams can't be underestimated. Often from their earliest years we get angry with our children for not fitting in to our stereotypes of how they are supposed to be. Letting go of assumptions—all girls will like to cook, or be neat and clean, all boys will want to be noisy and sporting—is very important, or our kids will feel they have somehow failed us.

Learning that your child is lesbian or gay can crash a truck through some of your fondest hopes. We can say we don't care and, out of consideration for our daughters, convince ourselves that we don't mind one bit, but *acceptance* isn't just an effort of will, it's a process you have to go through—and that means grief for what you may have lost as well. It's useful to take some time reflecting on this, take a break either alone or together, and just begin to let go of all those half-submerged dreams of "the daughter you imagined" and the daughter as a real person. Write a journal. Take a few long walks. Allow yourself some time to let go of one reality and learn to welcome another.

Parents of a lesbian daughter may find that, with her agreement, they want to let their friends know. After all, we all want to be understood and known by our friends. Most will probably be comfortable and welcoming. However, it's possible, depending on the circles you move in, that some friends will be judgmental.

Pamela Du-Valle, the mom of a gay son, wrote movingly of this in a poem that includes this verse:

"... I will tell you now and it is up to you
To my son and myself I have to be true
If you do not accept myself and my son
Our friendship is over, over and done."

This fierce loyalty to one's offspring is a great attribute and must give enormous heart to her son.

Beyond the transitions of "coming out," lesbian girls will have the same issues as everyone else: Will I find love? Will I be treated with respect by those around me?

There are whole books on this topic, as well as organizations like Parents, Families, and Friends of Lesbians and Gays (PFLAG), that can

Continued

Finding Her Soul (Ten to Fourteen Years)   103

help you if you have a lesbian daughter. But for any parent, it's worth being well informed. Even if your daughter is straight, she will likely have lesbian friends who will appreciate your being supportive and unfazed.

A final note—lots of girls go through intense friendships in their teens and are very affectionate. These friendships are not usually sexual and are not a sign of sexual orientation one way or the other. (In more open societies, boys, too, have strong friendships like this as part of growing up.) There is a fashion now for boys at parties and so on to urge girls to "make out" in imitation of porn movies designed to titillate men. With all this craziness around, girls worry and get tense and may pull back from friendships needlessly. Encourage your daughter to be herself and be open with friends, talk about what they feel is and isn't comfortable. There are too many labels put on us all—we are all unique and no label ever describes us.

CHAPTER SIX

Preparing for Adulthood

(Fourteen to Eighteen Years)

Imagine a girl of fourteen. She's just entering high school. She's almost grown to her full height, and she's come through puberty. She is physically capable of having a baby. She is strong, coordinated, and quite smart. (A few hundred years ago—or in certain parts of the world today—she would be getting married now.) So, what do you think? Is she ready for womanhood?

The answer will be clear to anyone with a fourteen-year-old daughter. Probably not! The qualities that make up maturity are emerging at fourteen, *but like a failing light bulb, they flicker on and off.* One minute she can be kind and caring, but another minute she can be thoughtless and self-obsessed. She can make great promises but forgets to keep them. She can lose all perspective. She's very prone to peer pressure. She can be wildly overemotional.

None of this is her fault—an early-teenage girl's brain is still setting up its center of control in the prefrontal cortex, and it's like a "head office" that isn't finished yet. She can go there, but not for long. The part of her brain called the *amygdala*—the center of impulsive and emotional reactions—may take over in a flash if she is pressured, distracted, or stressed.

It's true that in a traditional society a girl often got married at fourteen, but in those societies, cast-iron rules about acceptable behavior shackled her and defined every second of her life. Today we seek a very different womanhood for our daughters—independent, not proscribed by gender roles, and equal in opportunity to any man. Achieving that kind of womanhood takes a little longer.

The years from fourteen to eighteen are a time of intense preparation because modern womanhood is tough. Your daughter will need to be self-reliant, a clear thinker, emotionally strong, good with people, and responsible for her own life. Even better still, she will have a sense of purpose and be attuned to what makes life meaningful and good. These are your final blessings to her, before you send her out into the future.

What Makes You an Adult?

Today we consider adulthood as beginning somewhere between the ages of eighteen and twenty-one. So by eighteen, a girl needs to be "there" in terms of being able to function independently and well. She can legally drive a car, work, have sex, and make her own choices in every way, so we have to make sure she can do so without damaging or killing herself or anyone else. But it's more than just staying out of trouble, a real adult has her own goals and purpose in life, she has figured out what is really important. So between fourteen and eighteen, this is what we aim for with our girls.

In this chapter, we'll tell you the stories of two young women who make the journey from girlhood to womanhood. One is the survivor of a serious accident, the other is a famous singer who almost lost her career, until she was able to work out why she was in the world. For all girls, hopefully in less dramatic ways, the same lessons have to be learned: "Your life is in your hands. Other people's lives are in your hands. Welcome to the terrifying freedom of adulthood!"

Initiation into Womanhood

Old societies knew a lot about raising the young. They did things that only now our best neuroscience is proving right. For example, they deeply loved and indulged their babies and young children, delighting in them and letting them play and be unfettered. They expected much more of their six to twelve-year-olds, giving them jobs and responsibilities, and they always, without exception, put a lot of energy into their midadolescents, kick-starting them, exploding them almost, into adulthood. Becoming an adult was never left to chance.

There has been a lot of interest in recent years in the idea of parents and other caring adults creating adolescent "rites of passage." A rite of passage is a time of intensified activity, teaching, ritual, and involvement that says to a girl, "We will help you and celebrate you in becoming a woman."

In Australian schools, programs like the Rite Journey and Pathways to Womanhood are becoming widespread. These programs take the girls out of their usual world, to a place where they can spend time over several days with older women, including their mothers, female mentors, and teachers. The girls listen to stories about womanhood from these women, and are invited to make declarations of their own identity and values. The adults praise and affirm the girls' positive qualities, what they see in them, and invite them to say good-bye (and thank you) to girlhood.

Suffused through this is a sense of pride and honor in being a woman, a sense that has often disappeared from girls' views of themselves, with tragic consequences. At the end of these programs, the girls reenter the normal world, and as part of this, their fathers greet them in a ceremony that acknowledges they are now women, not girls.

Whether we participate in a formal program or simply take on the challenge ourselves as the parents and family of a girl, the same elements have to be there.

The question that we have to challenge our daughters with at this age boil down to this: "What kind of woman do you want to be?" A girl may answer in many different ways:

"I am true and trustworthy with my friends."

"I am in this world to help others."

"I am a leader and want to take people to a better world."

"I am a creator and want to make beauty."

"I am proud of being different and unique."

The dangers of being a woman need to be honestly discussed and put in perspective. Childhood is protected; womanhood is not. As one girl put it to me, "It's no longer my parents ruining up my life. I am free now to ruin my own life!"

A girl who has had a rite of passage isn't fully a woman yet, she is a *beginning woman*. But she has crossed the river, her sights are set on the future, and she is not going back.

Even Chores Teach You to Be Adult

Rites of passage are just the tip of the iceberg of growing up. Underneath lies all the work that mothers and fathers do to teach the joys of being a helpful and eventually an equal contributor around the house and in the community. Parents have to make this happen for one important reason: nobody would grow up if they didn't have to.

It's not done out of meanness or just a wish to get help with cooking, running errands, or paying the bills! These certainly matter, but it's what they represent and teach. Doing things for others creates an inner shift. We make the dinner, or keep our room a clean, neat and functional place. We earn money on the weekends to pay for some of our bills, and on the inside we feel proud, capable, and free.

Expect a lot of repetitive and careful teaching to take place around daily living. Do this with optimism and empathy rather than nagging or whining. Be patient and empathic (but insistent). You are her coach, and you have to be "welcome inside her head" for your message to really embed: "I know you're tired, but let's get started, and we can soon have it done. Then we can all take it easy."

You can help your daughter (or son) hugely by simply making sure they always do these things:

* Put away, wash, or tidy up what they have used.

* Keep their stuff in order so they can find things easily when needed.

* Have good manners and speak respectfully to people, whether strangers or family.

* Treat other people's property with respect.

* Apologize when they have done the wrong thing, make amends, and fix the problem they have caused.

Teenagers who don't pull their weight and let others clean up after them create a negative energy that saps everyone's happiness, including their own. The knack is to develop the habit of doing it right so that it's automatic, and there is no energy expended or doubt needed. You can get on with having a great time because the environment is efficient, clean, and easy to be in. It's so much easier to start this way and just keep it happening.

Of course, this is just the day-to-day stuff, also waiting out there is the big world. That takes it all to a whole new level.

Responsibility—The Toughest Lesson There Is

Marielle, age fourteen, was a happy and athletic girl. She was the oldest of four children and attended a co-ed high school in the western suburbs of Sydney, Australia. One spring afternoon, she and her friends poured laughing and chatting through the school gates and out toward the train station to travel home. They crossed at a pedestrian light just outside the school in a large group, just as they had every single day. But this time, they barely had time to turn their heads as the screech of brakes came microseconds before a large car plowed into them. One girl was killed instantly, another five, including Marielle, were seriously injured.

Marielle was in hospital for almost six months. Multiple operations reconstructed her body, painful and intense rehabilitation had her able to walk, and while she will never be quite as able-bodied again, she can live a normal life. Except for one thing: she is terrified of going anywhere near a road. She has agoraphobia and suffers nightmares and flashbacks. She can be driven to school, but it's an ordeal for her and her parents.

Her parents sought out counseling for her with a woman counselor in her fifties who specializes in trauma. Over several months, Marielle was taught relaxation and mindfulness skills, worked through what happened, and built up her mental strength. She improved considerably, but she is still not able to go near a road that has cars on it. If she tries, she begins to tremble uncontrollably, feels nauseated, and suffers attacks of diarrhea. These are the same symptoms that combat soldiers often suffer when they return home from war or a dangerous tour of duty: posttraumatic stress disorder.

Marielle's counselor is a very capable and creative woman who has become like a kind of feisty aunt to Marielle, able to soothe her but also to push her when needed. She is ready with the next step. They have been meeting for more three months. (I would not advise the following strategy ever be used unless a relationship is strong and well established.).

"Marielle, we've talked about what happened on that day, you've gradually pieced it together."

"Yes."

"There's something else we haven't talked about."

"Mmm?"

"When you talk about or think about the accident that happened that day, who do you blame?"

"The driver, the stupid idiot that killed my friend, that smashed me up."

(Marielle's words are angry, but her look is sad, she is tearing up now, as she often does when she talks about it.)

"Okay, so you think the driver was 100 percent to blame?"

"Yes."

"And you were an innocent victim of that?"

"Yes, and unlucky, too."

The counselor pauses, draws a deep breath. "Do you feel you have any share in the blame?"

There is a kind of booming silence. This question is a jolting one, and though she does not show it, Marielle's mind reels. "What do you mean?"

"You crossed on a red light . . ."

"Yes. We always look. It'd be stupid not to."

"Was there anything else you could have done?"

There is a pause. "How do you mean?"

The counselor is silent. The pair know each other well now; this turn of conversation could not have been taken without very considerable rapport.

Marielle finally speaks. "I still don't know what you mean."

"Did you look to see if there was a car coming?"

"We didn't need to. The light told us we could walk."

"So you didn't look?"

Marielle just stares back at the counselor. Their eyes lock, but inside her brain, wheels are spinning.

In the weeks that follow, Marielle plunges into another layer of dealing with what life has dealt her. The victim position was so easy to take; she was a child, innocently crossing at a light, with dozens of schoolmates with her. They could not have expected a car to speed into them, but they did not check—and a car did.

Who could allocate the responsibility in this? The driver was 100 percent responsible, and was in jail as a result, but Marielle suddenly grasped that she had been too trusting, too unaware of her environment, too distracted to really check she was safe. Cars don't always stop at red lights. Not all drivers are sane or sober. She *should* have looked.

Of course, part of Marielle knew this, as did everyone around the situation, but no one said so. Who would have had the heart to add blame to the suffering she had already gone through? But this counselor knew that the truth mattered, and that Marielle knew that, too.

Momentarily, Marielle plunged into the opposite extreme, from "no blame" to "all the blame." She agonized that she could have saved her friend's life if she had just been more alert. But the counselor was ready for this, and they continued to evaluate, drawing now on the strong bond of trust to do some tough talking.

"You trusted the drivers to do the right thing, because they always did. The light was red. That always worked in the past. But you can't trust all drivers. You should have looked. So should every other girl on that crossing. It might not have saved them. But it might have."

Gradually, Marielle took on her own sliver of responsibility, no more, no less. In a deeper sense, this was a lesson called "growing up." It was timely; at fourteen, a girl really is entering womanhood, and part of being an adult is knowing that the world is random and cruel, and you have to watch your back. You can hugely improve your safety by being wide awake and savvy.

In the weeks that followed, the lesson became not just a thought but a part of Marielle's body, too. The horrible injuries she had sustained had been contributed to, in just a small part, by her own behavior. She could change that behavior. She could be less a victim and more the agent of her own fate. Taking even 5 percent of the blame was a painful lesson, but an empowering one, too. Cars *are* dangerous, but much more so if you don't watch out for them. Somehow, along with this realization, Marielle's fear went away. She began to approach roads, not with her head down and trembling, but with a fierce eye on what was going on.

Marielle now goes over that crossing, and much more besides, with just a flicker, just a brief moment, of quiet determination, staring down death, knowing that death is always right alongside us. She is glad to be alive, determined to stay that way. She is not just healed, she is grown up.

The Real Secret of Adulthood

Now it's time for a very advanced idea. This is deep water, but I hope you will go there with me. I have come to believe that the biggest difference between an adult and a child is knowing *why* you are in the world.

Consider this for a moment: a child is in the world for him- or herself. That's appropriate and right, but it's not our ultimate goal. The highest happiness, according to both ancient wisdom and the most modern research in positive psychology, comes when we step outside our own importance and learn how to care for the big picture— the big life, not just our own small life.

This can easily be mistaken (especially given the history of women's lives) for being a martyr and living only for others. That's not what I am saying here.

There is a place where our own deepest needs—what we really love to do—intersect with the needs of the world we live in. When we find that place, it's all pure joy. The following story will help you to understand what I mean.

A Singer Finds Her Soul

Missy Higgins is an Australian musician and singer who is acclaimed worldwide for the raw beauty and authenticity of her songs. This talented woman started young; she signed a worldwide record deal when she was still a senior in high school. The songs on her first album had been hammered out on the practice piano in the school's music room. Then, suddenly, she was on a world stage. But the meteoric fame and exposure left her staggering, overwhelmed by panic attacks, and physically incapable of going on stage.

There had been warning signs earlier, including a hospitalization in her junior year after a nervous collapse. It was then that she learned that her father had also suffered from depression throughout his life, which he had managed to overcome.

Missy withdrew from performing completely, instructing her agent to send no offers, no invitations, or even to email, which he abided by for almost two years. She spent time in ashrams, traveled widely, saw a therapist, went to college, and worked hard to heal her life from the implosive forces of too much success too soon on a vulnerable and open heart.

It wasn't an easy time—a soul journey is never easy—but then something happened. Perhaps it was chance, or perhaps it was the natural result of all those sincere attempts to journey toward the truth. Acting on instinct, her agent broke his silence and sent her an invitation to perform at an all-women festival called Lilith Fair, in the United States. Something inside her said, "Yes, do this."

Her performance was awesome. Afterward, grateful fans surrounded her, thanking her warm-heartedly for what her music had given them over the years. She suddenly realized that the musical gift she had was for *other* people, that she had something to offer to the human race.

She has gone back to writing, recording, and performing her songs. I suspect this is something that all true, enduring performers have to realize: "it's not about me." The anxiety and pressure to succeed, the sense of exposure and vulnerability, somehow dissolve when you realize you stand in grace, and that you are there to give love to your listeners.

The meaning of art is to lift up your fellow human beings to a higher place. It's precious and special, and you have to honor it. Self is lost in the joining. This is what we mean by soul.

By eighteen, or twenty, or twenty-five, whenever it comes, a girl arrives at somewhere awesome: the beginning of womanhood. She knows that she holds the reins of her own life. She knows that the key to happiness is not in self-seeking. She feels connected to life and that she has a part to play in the human race. The real adventure can begin.

Teenage Girls and Sleep

Recently researchers have confirmed what parents always knew—that teenagers don't get enough sleep. Part of the problem is that the sleep cycle shifts in adolescence so that they actually need to sleep in longer. But we inevitably have to wake them to go to school. The accumulated sleep debt is bad for both learning and mental health, but there are remedies.

Australia's foremost adolescent psychologist and mental health campaigner, Dr. Michael Carr Gregg, explains:

It's 8.30 a.m. and we are standing outside a typical girls' school anywhere in the world. As students emerge from cars and buses, an ocean of sleepy faces appear before us, some grasping carry-out lattes in their hands—it's narcolepsy central.

Within half an hour, some of these young ladies will have their heads on desks, fast asleep, while others will be so sleep-deprived that they are oblivious to the learning going on around them.

It's official, teenagers—boys and girls—are the most sleep-deprived segment of the population. The world's leading authority in teenage sleep, Professor Mary Carskadon of Brown University in Rhode Island, found that on average adolescents get about 7.5 hours sleep on school nights, but 25 percent get 6.5 hours *or less*. That's a quarter of all teens ending up seriously sleep deprived. Carskadon found that in order for a young person to be optimally alert, they require *9.25 hours* of sleep. It is increasingly evident to educators and psychologists that night after night, many girls are treating sleep as an optional extra and are building colossal sleep debts.

If you attached an electroencephalograph to those dozing girls, heads down on their desks, you'd see that 50 percent will go directly into REM sleep, exhibiting the same brain waves as patients with narcolepsy. These girls don't actually have narcolepsy; nevertheless, they're living under conditions that actually make them appear as if they do.

Insufficient sleep not only impacts on girls' physical health, but also dramatically reduces their capacity to perform and respond appropriately while sitting in a classroom, driving a car, playing a sport, or interacting with adults. It increases rates of depression, and even increases suicidal feelings and thoughts. From an academic point of view, a good night's sleep is the most powerful study aid there is.

Schools must start teaching "bed-ucation" because adolescents need to know how a lack of sleep impacts on the 100 billion brain cells and one trillion connections. Parents need to make sleep a priority and set limits and boundaries around bedtime from an early age. Finally, perhaps we need to start reviewing the issue of school starting time. Studies have found that a starting time for high school of even half an hour later creates a marked gain in health and well-being, as well as learning.

What to Do?
Have an evening routine and clear bedtimes. Reading in bed to chill out for half an hour is fine, but do not allow electronic media—phones, iPads, computers, or TVs—in bedrooms (screens affect the brain's readiness for sleep, apart from the content being too stimulating).

Teens may need to sleep in on weekends to clear their sleep debt. This is a healthy catch-up, but it's better if they get nine hours a night during the week.

Because of the time shift in adolescence, schools should not start too early. We need to change school schedules to suit teenagers' bodies better.

Dreaming Forward

This chapter ends the five stages of growing a girl into a woman. As a way to finish up, let's do some dreaming. Whatever age your girl is now, it's great to glimpse and even begin to aim for the woman she will become. So settle back in your chair or pillow, and come on a journey . . .

You are in a peaceful house, on a leafy street. It's evening, and still warm after a sunny summer's day. You are older but still strong and well. You glance out of your window and see out on the road that a car is pulling up. It's an electric car, silent, compact, and sleek.

Stepping out of the car is a young woman. As you look closer you realize it's your grown-up daughter. How does she look? What kind of clothes is she wearing?

Does she have a partner with her? Children? You go out to greet her. Can you see what kind of person she is, what qualities shine from her? How has she changed? What is her voice like? How tall is she? Is she fit and well? What kind of things has she been doing with her time and talents? Let your imagination fill in the details.

Bring her inside your house, sit down, and talk. What is she telling you? How are you feeling? See the connections between the childhood you gave her and the strengths and qualities she now has. Feel proud and deeply satisfied. A fine woman will live on after you are gone, and she will pass on what you have taught and given her down the generations.

In a Nutshell

* Preparing a girl for womanhood requires a lot of teaching in the years from fourteen to eighteen.
* Rites of passage are needed to make the leap. It doesn't happen without help.
* Work and responsibility are a necessary part of training to be an adult.
* Marielle learned from a terrible accident that she holds the reins of her own life.
* A talented singer found peace in giving. Adulthood means escaping from the prison of self and being part of the big life.
* You can't form good relationships until you are strong in your own right.
* The age of eighteen is not womanhood, but it is the start of womanhood.

PART TWO

Hazards and Helps:

The Five Big Risk Areas and How to Navigate Them

CHAPTER SEVEN

Too Sexy Too Soon

During the four years I was working on this book, I talked to everyone I met about what they thought was happening to girls. Hairdressers, cab drivers, and people seated beside me on planes were soon plunging into the topic. Friends, family, and colleagues all said the same thing: girls are growing up too fast.

The signs are familiar to every parent. Most eight-year-old girls are already worried about their figure. There are twelve-year-olds who won't go outside without putting on makeup. Magazines aimed at ten- to fourteen-year-olds discuss oral sex. We seem to have just let this happen, without asking if it's a good idea. But clearly it's not.

I have a friend, a feisty and tireless young woman, who is a campaigner for the mental health of girls. She visits schools and talks to the girls about the pressures in their lives. One day she received this letter:

You don't know me. I was just one of those girls in the audience today. But it was like you were speaking just to me.

Until today, I thought that because I have small breasts, I would have to get breast implants to be a real woman. Also, until today, I believed what my friends said—that if I hadn't had sex by the time I was sixteen, I was a loser.

After hearing you, and all you had to say, I don't think those things anymore. I feel so happy and strong. You told me that I am all right, just as I am. Until I heard you, I never believed that.

I am crying as I write this. I can't thank you enough for your message and for giving it to all girls like me.

This letter is at the same time inspiring, sad, and infuriating. Our daughters should, after forty years of feminism, feel free to choose, to be themselves. They should know deep in their bones that they are valuable and unique. Yet girls have never been more insecure. How they look, and their "hotness," has become a constant obsession. Some girls think of little else.

Relationships–How Young Is Too Young?

The most important message of human development is that you can't jump stages. You can't put the roof on until you've built the walls. We mess up girls when we race them into needs and behavior that they are not yet neurologically ready for. Most fourteen- to eighteen-year-old girls are still forming their identities. Imagine if a fifteen-year-old gets into an intense relationship with a boy. At this age, she is not yet sure of who she is, and so there is a strong chance that she will look to the boy to define her (and vice versa).

She is not yet very secure, so she may cling, fret, and worry that he won't like her. Any sign of disinterest will put her in a spin. She won't clearly know what she likes and wants other than what he likes and wants. If he is the same age, he might have the same problem. If he is older, he will find it hard not to automatically call the shots and develop a power relationship where he decides everything that happens. (Girls who lack good fathering often mix up father needs with boyfriend needs and get into this kind of relationship.)

Girls of fourteen or sixteen often have boyfriends. It's nice to have someone special in your life, but it's also emotionally hazardous, and not likely to last very long. If it becomes sexual, it can break hearts very easily and leave baggage for future relationships. Taking it slow is a really good idea.

Being evaluated in terms of how pleasing you are to others, how you rate as a "product" has taken girls back fifty years. *Sexualization—* the forcing of a sexual identity onto someone from the outside, was a term originally applied in cases of child sexual abuse. Today it's a problem seen in every elementary school. It isn't new, but it's much stronger, and more pervasive. Few girls escape it.

How Happy Sexuality Grows by Itself

Let's talk about how it's meant to be. Left to themselves, all young people grow in sexual awareness as puberty wakes them to this new phase of life. It happens slowly; there is a natural reticence or embarrassment that keeps things at a manageable pace.

Just one example of this is that preteen and midteen girls are often crazy about boy bands or singers who are not sexual in any way, perhaps because this allows a manageability and gentleness in their feelings that lets them feel safe and private.

Girls go from barely tolerating boys in their preteens, to finding them interesting but annoying in midteens, to gradually finding one or two boys they can relate to enjoyably as good friends as they

The Three Ls

It's not unusual to be attracted to someone you don't even like, who you would hate to be around. Hormones are like that sometimes. It helps to teach your daughter about the "three Ls": *liking, loving,* and *lusting*—each of which is quite different. Feeling all three toward one person is what we all hope for, but at the very least we need to know which is which. Confusing lust for love, loving for liking, or liking for lust all create serious problems. Mothers and fathers can talk about these things in a lighthearted but serious way; girls will need to have a handle on this because it will hugely affect their success at having happy relationships.

mature. With any luck, they are able to mix in groups and get more practiced at talking, and check out boys' different characters under a range of circumstances. If they encounter a boy who is funny and kind, able to have a conversation, who doesn't put them or other people down, they may find themselves wanting to pair up and go out.

When relationships begin, they do so with a lot of caution and testing out. In fact, young love is all about exploration, two people gradually unfolding their intimacy as trust grows. It's one of the sweetest times of life, you feel intensely alive and the world seems like a beautiful place.

This is where the sexualization of kids does the most harm. Hammered by media about the need to be sexy, seeing role models on TV and in movies who separate sex from any kind of relationship aspects, believing that sex is the way to get love, kids now behave not as they *want*, from their inner signals, but as they feel they *should*.

They believe that if they don't deliver, their partner will go elsewhere. When they have sex they are not relaxed or excited, but deeply anxious about how they are performing, wondering how they compare to others, and what tricks they are supposed to carry out. A part of life that is meant to be beautiful and life changing has been stolen from this generation. It's a terrible loss.

When interviewed by researchers, girls revealed that much of the sex they were having was in order to keep boys happy. Many found it empty or unsatisfying. Like the "lay back and think of England" attitudes of a century ago, these girls are resigned to sex being a necessity. Many girls drink a lot of alcohol on nights out with boys just to make it easier, less personal.

Having sex with lots of different partners is not good for your body. While the use of condoms has greatly improved, many girls are on the pill and so don't see the need. Girls are now suffering soaring levels of infections, including chlamydia, which may affect their fertility, and the upsurge of oral sex is leading to a far greater incidence of mouth and throat cancers.

Preventing our daughters from being brainwashed down this road of "too sexy too soon" has to start early, if possible. The media that comes into your house is a great place to begin.

The Facts

When researchers at Melbourne's Latrobe University carried out their recurring large-scale survey of teenage sexuality in 2002 and again in 2008, they found something quite alarming. It galvanized those of us who work with teens and shocked us. The survey found that the percentage of girls who had had sex with multiple partners while still at school had *doubled* in six years. Taken across a wider timescale—going back thirty years—that group had grown from about 4 percent to 20 percent of all girls, and showed no sign of slowing down. By the time you read this, it will likely be even higher. Multiple partners was defined as three or more—by the age of seventeen.

Stopping the Toxic Flood

Although we don't like to admit it, we human beings are herd animals. Being intensely social, we take our cues from those around us as to what is normal, but today those cues come not so much from real people as from media: TV, movies, music videos, and magazines. In the last fifty years, and especially the last ten, we have shifted from spending hours a day with family, relatives, and friends to spending much more time isolated in our houses or rooms. Some commentators believe that today's girls only have *one-fifth* as much time with caring older adults compared to fifty years ago. When Grandma lived down the road and several aunties or of Mom's friends lived in the same small town, girls had lots of "wise woman" talk in their lives.

Today that's all changed. We watch TV instead of spending time with real friends and family. (TV has almost *become* our family; jovial, nonthreatening men and reassuringly maternal women join us at breakfast, just as Mom and Dad once did in the old days.)

We adults use TV for entertainment, but our kids use it for quite a different purpose: to find out what is *normal* behavior. Of course, what they see is far from normal. With each passing year, TV programming has to be more and more sexually explicit, more violent, more rude and abusive, more emotionally intense, to hold our interest. The characters have to be more ravishingly good looking and "hot" to keep people watching. So what is normal on TV is wildly at odds with real life.

Many kids' favorite shows are "reality" programs. These often feature immature young adults in situations of contrived flirtation, rejection and hurt, bullying and exclusion. Kids know all about rejection and exclusion, and so they watch, mesmerized. They see competitive and nasty behavior, selfishness and cruelty portrayed as normal. They think the world must be like this—a big and heartless place where no one cares. If you are not pretty enough or sexy enough, you won't be chosen.

There are many other changes. When we were kids, children's viewing was very defined. Today it is all blurred—horrific news items interrupt afternoon viewing, crass and offensive behavior is in so-called family shows. (A classic is *Two and a Half Men*, which has a child included in its cast, and the running joke is his exposure to the sexual exploits of the "grownups.")

Can't We Just Teach Them to Resist?

It's not that there is any one terrible instance of media harm; it's the relentless, damaging flood of material. Inch by inch, kids are progressively brainwashed about what it is normal to think, feel, look like, and do. They can be helped to resist some of this, but it's *really* hard work. The experts who advise us to "discuss the media with your children, help them to deconstruct the messages, and be media aware" are not wrong, and we should do this. But so much of the effect is unconscious, and it just keeps coming.

TV and magazine ads have an especially insidious influence on girls. The market in selling useless things to preteen and midteen girls is worth billions of dollars each year across the globe. These purchases are things that girls never needed or thought of in earlier generations—makeup, skin and hair products, fashion and footwear that piles up in closets. Twenty years ago, a teenage girl would go downtown happily in jeans and a clean T-shirt. Today it takes an hour of anxious preparation before she will go out in public. Even toys and games for little girls are about fashion, beauty, modeling, and being sexy.

The aim of advertising is to attack your mental health—to worry you and make you discontent so you're vulnerable to a sales pitch. If you want to sell products to a girl, whether she is four or fourteen, you first have to make her *insecure*—about her looks, friends, clothes, weight, skin, and hair. Everything about her is an opportunity to fail.

TV, magazines, billboards, and music videos pour this "lookism" message onto girls wherever they turn. The result: appearance has become the primary concern of children who should have never given it a second thought.

Clothes were once worn to keep the wind out! Now mothers complain that it's almost impossible to buy girls' clothing for preteens or teens that isn't revealing or, as one put it, slutty. I couldn't help smiling when a colleague who counsels sex workers told me there was real annoyance among her clients that they no longer could be identified in the streets because seventeen-year-olds dressed and looked just like them.

Nip and Tuck

At a recent talk I gave in Sydney, Australia, a group of young women doctors cornered me after the show. They told me that they were receiving frequent requests from teenage girls for plastic surgery on their labia. These girls had seen porn movies or photos and were deeply concerned that they looked "untidy," and they wanted to be tidied up.

What Can We Do?

Let's tackle the easy issues first. Television stands out like the Mount Everest of media intrusion into children's lives. While the Internet takes over more in the teen years, TV is your child's teacher for thousands of hours of their formative years. It's there in the corner of the living room, sometimes in many other rooms as well. It's like a third parent.

What does it teach? Researchers have identified six key messages:

1. Your looks are the most important thing about you.
2. Your physical characteristics (shape, weight, skin, hair, teeth, color, smell) are *never ever* good enough.
3. Sex is something that you exchange for love and attention, or for power. It's primarily a currency.
4. It's normal and fine to have sex with people you don't even know or especially like.
5. The world is a scary, lonely, dangerous, and competitive place. Better get going—you might lose the race.
6. The answer to all life's problems is to buy something.

If you agree with these messages, that's fine. You, your partner, and the TV are all of one accord. If you don't agree, though, you have to act.

STEP 1: NO TV IN BEDROOMS

All the research from around the world shows that kids with their own TV see far more unsuitable material and do so without the awareness or discussion with you, their parents.

This causes harm to them. They are much more prone to anxiety, they have measurably poorer sleep, and do less well at school. If you have TVs in your kids' bedrooms, take them away now!

STEP 2: CONSCIOUSLY DECIDE WHAT YOU VIEW

You need to decide where your family will be on the TV-using spectrum. Some families don't even have TV. About 3 percent of families make this choice at present, and it's growing. Their kids are more creative, settled, do better at school, and have far wider interests.

Next, some families have taken the American Pediatric Association's guidelines on board and don't have TV for the under-threes. (The APA found that TV has no benefits for and in fact causes significant harm to babies and toddlers, diminishing their language development and stressing them, reducing their activity levels, even affecting their vision by being at a fixed focal length when toddlers need to be looking far and near.)

The People We Worry About

There is a pattern that a great many families have with television—they have it on *all* the time. The first to wake up turns it on, the last to go to bed turns it off. In these families, some distinct things happen:

1. Nobody ever has a good conversation—either long or deep—because you can't when people have divided attention. So it just doesn't happen. "Always On" families don't talk much. They grumble a lot though.

2. The kids absorb thousands of messages—bewildering, random, scary, distorted, artificial, and just plain wrong—about life and the world. People who watch a lot of TV are found to be much more anxious, depressed, fearful, inattentive, and powerless than those who don't. And as many a parent has tried to explain to a terrified three-year-old who just saw something they shouldn't, "It isn't real." But to them it's more real than life. After all, it's on the TV.

Would you invite scary adults into your house to make your children anxious and pressure them to buy things they don't need for problems they don't have? As a parent, you are in charge of the emotional safety of your home. You have to decide what comes through your door, and through your television. TV wants to own your daughter's mind; you mustn't let it.

Some families have TV but use only DVDs and prerecorded favorite shows, discovering that small kids often love to watch the same shows many times, getting familiar with the dialogue and songs. This way they can eliminate ads, the jumpy interruptions, and scary news breaks or promos that occur on almost all stations.

Many families, with kids at any age, have started to have their TV on only for specific shows, chosen by each child, perhaps for half an hour a day each. It's never just left running.

Magazines

The same goes for magazines, especially fashion magazines and girls' magazines, which are bursting at the seams with ads for makeup and clothes. Don't buy them. There are some great alternatives.

Girls' magazines have occasional bursts of trying to clean up their act. One has recently stopped using airbrushed images; another stopped running its "model quest," then brought it back. Sometimes these publications run worthwhile articles and have a good advice column, but their reason for existing is advertising, so they aren't going to stop their primary harm, which is making girls not like themselves as they *are*. That wouldn't sell much merchandise. Advertising is the misery industry—it makes you less happy with yourself and your life. Girls really don't need any help with this.

Then there's the content. Which boys are hot. How to *be* hot. Hotness competitions. We could go on, but you get the idea.

To sum up, you can choose the media that comes into your home, and you can start right away. If your daughters are little, you can make a huge difference. If they are older, it's still not too late. You can also do the other things in this book: raise their sense of being loved and special, with an identity built on what they *do* not how they look. You can build their sense of community and belonging with other adults and activities so there are lots of buffers to their believing in themselves. It all works together; you just have to have your eyes open.

Girls and Desire—What Should You Teach Your Daughter?

Reading the many discussions of teenage girls and sex, you could start to feel that it's all about trouble. So it's extremely important to keep a true perspective—that sex is a beautiful, exciting, and health-giving thing, and that girls ought to own it, enjoy it, and revel in it.

Girls have every bit as much desire and yearning as their boy counterparts. We parents, especially mothers, need to tell our girls long before the anxieties have time to get a hold that sex is great, and they are going to love it.

Deborah Tolman, at the Center for Research on Women at Wellesley College, carried out some stunning interviews with girls for her book *Dilemmas of Desire*. She found a concerning thing: When teen girls talked about sex, they emphasized the *negatives*. More than that, they frequently sounded weak and passive in describing sexual experiences they had already had. This could be best summed up in the phrase, "It just happened." Being with a boy they are not really sure they like, having a bit too much to drink, and sex "happening" seems almost the norm. This was how they experienced it—not a lot of choice, not a lot of desire, no real intention, and no real sense of agency (being the active one and seeking and getting a wonderful time). There wasn't a lot of "I wanted . . ." or "I loved . . ." or "I enjoyed . . ." in their language.

This really needs to be improved. As much as adults worry about teenagers being too sexual, there is a paradoxical thing that Tolman and others, including myself, have come to believe: girls who are in touch with their own sexual desires, and comfortable to acknowledge and express them, are better able to choose whether or not to have sex, with whom, and under what circumstances.

Too often in the past, parents and society have sent a message that there are only two kinds of girls: "bad" girls who presumably love sex, and "good" girls who presumably don't. This sets girls up for having a bad time. If a girl feels desire, she might label this as bad and suppress it. Or a girl wanting to be rebellious might have sex when really she doesn't

Continued

want to—it's just a way to make a statement or get some affirmation that she is interesting and worthwhile. It all gets very messy.

Talking about this might not be where every mother-daughter's relationship is at, but it's worth working for. Some teenagers don't like talking about sex with parents, but we need to make sure someone is talking to them. Sometimes aunties or older women friends can affirm this more comfortably for girls than their moms can. Tolman said in her book, "Every girl I interviewed said that no adult woman had ever talked to her before about sexual desire and pleasure 'like this,' that is, so overtly, specifically, or in such depth." Perhaps we should.

In a Nutshell

* Mainstream media, half by accident, half by intent, is making sex seem compulsory for girls at increasingly younger ages.

* It damages teen girls by sexualizing them when they are not equipped or ready.

* Young love is being trashed by making it performance laden, shallow, and rushed.

* Girls are now much more anxious about their looks, clothes, and fitting in.

* Because this starts very young, we can make a big difference by not having much or any television in small children's lives. We can choose which magazines and other media to buy. We can talk to our daughters and foster an empowered and conscious sense of their sexuality that is special and personal— not a commodity.

* Girls' magazines generally do more harm than good.

* All the positive things you do to give your daughter connections and interests will set her free to have a happy and enthusiastic sex life when she is ready, and by her own choice.

CHAPTER EIGHT

Mean Girls

It's not a grimy or mean school—there are trees and fields all around, and nice houses in the distance—but something has taken over the girls. They stand in a ring of about ten, and keep the newcomer in the middle from getting away. They are calling her names and moving in closer, pushing her. Her face is streaked with tears. Eventually it stops, and they disperse, but the memory will stay with this girl for years, sometimes waking her from sleep.

Bullying is in the news, and it seems to be happening everywhere— in the adult world as well as in the world of children. Experts do not think it's an epidemic, but rather that at last people have really had enough of it and are speaking up. Bullying is being called what it is, and that's the first step to ending it.

Among girls, bullying is most often done in nonphysical ways— name calling, spreading nasty rumors online, excluding or embarrassing a girl by pulling faces or rolling eyes to make her feel stupid. This is sometimes called "relational aggression," which is to say that just because you aren't getting hit, doesn't mean it doesn't hurt.

Physical bullying still happens, too, especially among younger girls and, of course, from boys. At any one time, bullying affects one in five children worldwide, and is so severe in some cases that it has caused suicides, shootings, and knifings, but above all real misery for millions of boys and girls. It is something we have to address.

Small but Strong

This story was told to me by a mother in Wellington, New Zealand. Her daughter, Kiri, age seven, was the smallest in her class, a lively and quick-minded girl who loved school. One day Kiri came home very upset. She sobbed in her mother's arms, would not eat her evening meal, but refused to talk about what had made her so unhappy. Then, later that night, she finally told her dad about it.

A much larger girl at school had for several weeks been picking on her, pushing her out of games with her friends, and then taking her place. It was annoying, and scary, and more than once the girl had really hurt her arms by squeezing her hard. But the biggest hurt was the feeling of powerless humiliation. That's why she found it so hard to tell her family.

Kiri's dad and mom emailed the head of the school that night, labeling the email as a "complaint" so that it was formal and would have to be taken notice of. The next day her dad phoned for an appointment and met with the principal that same afternoon. The principal interviewed each of the girls in that social group to get more of the picture. He then met with the girl who was doing the bullying and Kiri together and asked the girl to apologize and promise to stop. Rather graciously, Kiri said that it had not happened as much lately.

Under this much scrutiny and with the impact of the interview (which was done in a thoughtful way and not punitive or angry in tone), the bullying stopped.

It didn't escape Kiri's parents that it was her dad she had told about her problem. Kiri was one of five children, and her dad was quite a busy man, but he decided this was a kind of reaching out for him, and so he decided to do more with his daughter. He and Kiri started going swimming together at a center nearby. This was not something he or she had ever done before, and they both really enjoyed it. She gained confidence in deep water and began to enjoy swimming at school, too, because she was now more familiar with it. She also really loved the time with her dad. Kiri's sense of self-worth visibly grew.

In short, the response of everyone turned the situation into one that increased Kiri's confidence and turned the crisis into an opportunity to grow.

It Takes Three

There are always three parts to a bullying situation. First, the perpetrator. This is usually someone who is feeling badly about themselves, who gets to feel better by passing on their pain to someone else. Research into children who bully has found that they suffer more from depression and are also more prone to suicide in later life. The girl who bullied Kiri was a bit of a loner who was having a difficult time at home. It's likely this girl envied Kiri for her happiness and circle of friends, but also, since she was small, saw Kiri as someone she could easily push around.

The second part is the victim. Kiri did not deserve to be bullied, but she gained strength and it's likely she would speak up more for herself in future. The evidence suggests that it doesn't work to "hit back" with bullies—often they are bigger or there are a group of them—but verbally responding, being angry, and, of course, asking for help, as well as being definite about your rights to be not pushed around, all help.

Finally, there are the bystanders. If they speak up and object to the bullying, stand alongside the victim, and, if need be, tell others what is happening, bullying often stops. This is hard because sometimes girls feel that if they do this they will become the next victim. Talk to your daughter about how important it is to protect others who are less strong or confident and tell her what she can say to intervene, things like, "Hey, that's not fair," "She's my friend, leave her alone," and "Stop being stupid. You are hurting her," along with some confident body language.

In Kiri's case, the school responded well and gave the situation time and energy. The head of the school saw it as a chance to improve the connectedness between himself and the children, create a safer environment, and do it in a nonpunishing way. The staff also discussed how they could meet the needs of the bullying girl, too, because she was clearly having a hard time in her life.

The three-part solution is important. The "victim" becomes more confident, sometimes by receiving more long-term support and finding ways to develop her sense of power. In Kiri's case, this came from more one-to-one time with her dad. The "bully" becomes more aware of the feelings of others, but also of her own feelings—she may be in a lot of pain and need some real care. And the community around the problem—the school, or family, or workplace—is changed by people talking more honestly about what is happening and not just ignoring it.

Speaking Up

Rosalind Wiseman is world famous for her book about bullying and girls, called *Queen Bees and Wannabes*. Rosalind is like the auntie you always wanted—friendly, straight talking, and absolutely clear in her advice. She taught self-defense classes to girls for many years, and the girls often shared with her their social and personal problems with bullying and cliques. She now campaigns full-time "for dignity in how people treat each other."

Her advice is extraordinarily clear.

To a thirteen-year-old teased by a boy (using obscene language) about her breast size, she says, "Write down exactly what he says to you, and where and when, and your feelings about that. Get it all down. Take it to the smartest and best school counselor or teacher and administrator that you know at your school and ask them to help. You absolutely have the right to not be talked to like that."

An aunt and mother ask her about sexy text messages that their fourteen-year-old girl has been sending to boys. Wiseman dismisses the privacy concerns completely. "You own the mobile phone and pay the bills. You own that phone. But more than that, texting is not private. Anyone can read texts or pass them on. If you want to be private, use a diary. Texting is public behavior, and parents need to know about it."

While being very clear about the need to intervene, Wiseman is empathic with both sides of the situation. She points out that the girl wants to sound sexy, interesting, and grown-up to these boys. From her viewpoint, that's what she is doing. To the boys, it sounds like she is advertising her availability to actually do those things she is texting. Maybe this is true, or not, but it's a parent's job to intervene protectively. Parents have a better handle on consequences. They can do this sensitively and kindly, but with a clear boundary.

The Importance of Bystanders

Wiseman's work has also underscored the importance of bystanders. In 2011, she helped make a documentary for the NBC television program *Dateline*. In a powerful and revealing experiment, teenage girls were brought into the studio and left in a large room to choose clothes, supposedly for a segment about fashion choices.

Unknown to the others, three of the girls in each group were professional actors. On cue, two of them began to bully the third (in one instance about her weight, in another, about her choice of clothes) to see how the other girls would react—would they help, or would they join in? Meanwhile, their parents watched from another room.

What unfolded was powerful and moving—since almost all of us have been bullied in our lives, it's hard to watch without being affected. In some of the instances, the bystanders spoke up. One girl in particular was wonderful to watch, she simply would *not* allow the actors to speak rudely to the third girl. But in other instances, girls who were nervous and unsure of themselves actually joined in the laughter.

(A typical strategy of bullies is to recruit others into their "gang" as a prelude to picking on someone else, and it's easy for insecure girls to fall in with this behavior out of their own fear of exclusion.)

Their mothers cringed as they watched on a monitor in the next room and saw their daughters joining in the mockery and not doing anything to stop it.

But the final incident was the most touching. In the final group to go through the experiment, one girl could be seen on camera silently walking away and weeping. The film's producers immediately stopped and intervened. It emerged that this girl was being actively bullied at school in *real* life, by both girls and boys, who targeted her for being poor. She was physically afraid each day she went to school. She had not been able to tell her mother, because it would make her mom feel worse about their low income. It was a powerful moment as the mothers returned to the room, and it was all discussed. Rosalind Wiseman helped this girl (privately after the sessions) to learn to deal with her attackers, and the program reported that she had successfully stood up to a boy and a girl who had been ringleaders at her school. It was a stark reminder of how cruelty arises so easily, and needs to be dealt with—by bystanders first, but by adults as well in sending clear signals and always following through.

Everyone Experiences Bullying

It's important to understand that we *all* are bullies sometimes, we are all victims sometimes, and we are all bystanders sometimes who do or do not intervene. It's a natural and important part of getting along with others that we learn to assert what we need, express opinions, and stand up for ourselves.

It's important for your daughter to have some things to say when others push her around. "I don't like you doing that. You need to stop." A worldwide program called Rock and Water was developed after bullies actually killed a boy in Holland, and there was an outcry to make changes in schools. Rock and Water teaches kids skills such as how to stand at their full height, make strong eye contact, and walk away while looking back at the aggressor. It is a complete program in self-confidence and physical safety, but the essence of its message is "standing strong."

Teach your daughter to be able to say, "That's bullying, and that's not right." Of course, that won't always stop what's happening, but it's the first step. Name what is happening. "You're bullying her/me, that isn't right/that's so unfair/that's so uncool." If bullying continues, go and get help. Tell your daughter clearly that she has a right to be safe and respected, and make it real. Follow up with the school if need be, and don't stay at a school that doesn't take sufficient action. (Your child's school should have a program addressing bullying, making it clearly understood and identified, so everyone knows what to do and how to get help.)

The world has bullied women and girls as a group for thousands of years. Standing up for yourself as a girl is part of a historic change, too. That's another good reason to do it.

Cyberbullying

With the advent of social media—Facebook, texting, email, and Twitter—a whole new kind of bullying has been made possible. Sending horrible texts, and spreading rumors or cruel comments online has become widespread.

The worst thing is that girls who have their mobile phone or computer in their bedroom feel they should check on what's happening when they are at home or late at night when they're in bed. In the "good old days" before computers or smartphones, home was at least a haven of peace until the next day. The result is a lot of stress and sleeplessness.

It's a good idea to not allow digital media in bedrooms and to have a rule that all members of the family charge and leave their phones in the kitchen each night. But once again, messaging of a threatening or ugly kind should not just be kept private. Not responding to minor examples may cause it to stop, but if it persists or is especially nasty, it needs to be taken up with the school or the provider. Also, you don't have to make yourself available to it—change privacy settings, "unfriend" people who aren't being friendly, change your number, or get a new email address.

In an excellent movie about girls growing up, *The Descendants*, starring George Clooney, a distant dad is forced to care for his daughters after his wife has a boating accident. Early in the movie, his younger daughter is involved in sending mean texts to a girl at school about her weight. The girl's mother, a feisty Hawaiian, demands an apology from daughter and father. The cyberbullying was done out of a kind of blindness to its consequence—it just felt to her like a joke, shared by a group of friends. She realizes the harm she has done and is somewhat ashamed, but it helps that her father also is embarrassed and shows it, and is eager to fix it up.

Sometimes talking to the person doing it, or their parents, can be done in a reasonable and friendly way by you or by the school, and it can bring about some growing up.

Where Is This Meanness Coming From?

Maggie Hamilton, an Australian writer about girls' lives, has a very good explanation of how meanness has arisen in girl culture today. Maggie believes that girls who are deeply stressed by the pressure to conform to our highly competitive and insecure world begin to operate in survival mode, constantly anxious and hypervigilant. They don't get enough love at home, have grown up too fast, and are constantly on edge. As a result, they do not have the time or place for empathy or kindness.

Bullying expert Kate Hadwen and her team at Edith Cowan University in Perth, Western Australia, surveyed many thousands of children in schools across the state and found that about one in five bullies is not responsive to ordinary appeals to empathy. In other words, ordinary programs will not work with them. These kids will require long-term intervention and are at risk of both doing a lot of harm and ending up in a lot of trouble. This rather chilling fact means that adults have to be willing to intervene, as kids themselves will not be safe unless action is taken long-term to monitor the problem.

While the "mean girls" culture has received a lot of attention, it's important to realize that most school environments are not like that at all. When *Queen Bees and Wannabes* became a best seller, hundreds of girls wrote to Rosalind Wiseman to tell her they recognized exactly the world she described. But then something interesting happened—hundreds more girls and women wrote saying that their girlhood was *nothing* like this. It began to be clear that Wiseman was writing about a particular sector of America, the UK, and Australia, and every developed industrial nation that was not representative of the whole. At least, not yet.

Girls in these better environments still had friendship groups and some degree of status competition—the popular "cool" girls, the more study-oriented girls, the gentler more bohemian kids, and so on—but they were not by and large mean to each other. And the boundaries were more flexible; you could move about and, more importantly, you could be yourself. It was kinder and more happy and relaxed.

Often the mean girls are found more at the extremes of society— on the one hand, in the more affluent demographic but also the more competitive one, where parents are financially better off but are time poor and less engaged. These girls have smartphones and credit cards and sometimes their own cars, but they do not have a whole lot of love. By contrast, some meanness comes from serious poverty and hardship, where parents are too busy or absent, and aggression is a common coping device. But this is not always so; there are poor kids who are also very kind and rich kids who are protective and gentle. There is always freedom to choose what kind of person you will be.

In a Nutshell

* Bullying affects about one in five children—it's way too common and causes a lot of pain.

* Stopping bullying requires change in all three players: victim, perpetrator, and bystanders.

* The role of the bystanders is critical, and your daughter can learn to be one who prevents others from being bullied.

* Cyberbullying has become a problem because it can be done at a distance. Dealing with it involves shortening that distance by communicating the hurt and concern back to the perpetrator.

* Adults need to know about bullying and to act when it is occurring, but not in a way that makes it worse. Calm, friendly, but determined action is best.

* Some girl cultures are mean because of the lack of love in that demographic. There are plenty of girl cultures that are healthy and supportive.

CHAPTER NINE

Bodies, Weight, and Food

Does your daughter worry about her weight? Do you worry about yours? You aren't alone, because body image has become a worldwide obsession and people have never been more confused—or unwell. About 15 percent of all girls and women will experience an eating disorder at some time in their lives—it is a massive epidemic.

Not long ago I listened to two young women presenting a stunning analysis of what the science is telling us about health, food, and body size. Lydia Jade Turner and Sarah McMahon have backgrounds in clinical work with eating disorders, but they are also committed to changing the culture around diet obsession, and especially a diet industry that makes matters a whole lot worse. Lydia and Sarah agreed to write this special section for the book.

A Candle Burning at Both Ends
by Lydia Jade Turner and Sarah McMahon

Most countries around the world are facing a serious public health crisis over body weight, and that crisis has two extremes. On the one hand, approximately one-quarter of school-aged children are reported to be "overweight" or "obese." On the other, the National Eating Disorders Collaboration reports the frightening news that eating disorders have increased twofold in the past five years. While some parents are being pressured to put their children on diets, others are dealing with the horror of watching their daughters refuse to eat anything at all. The terrifying thing is that none of this is working. Despite all the antiobesity rhetoric, children are getting fatter, and despite warnings about eating disorders, more girls are falling prey to them. We are doing something wrong.

Leading health experts from many countries now believe that the problem arises from putting our focus on the wrong thing; we shouldn't be focused on weight, because weight is not as important as health. Their research shows that if we shift our focus onto health and enjoying eating and exercising our bodies, we would be far better off.

Why Dieting Is Harmful

You may be shocked to learn that fifty years of research has come to an astounding conclusion: dieting hardly *ever* works. Approximately 95 percent of all people who go on diets regain the weight lost within two to five years. There are no diets anywhere that do better than this. How many times have you heard a new diet claiming to be the one that will make you lose pounds if only you buy this book and this product? If this confuses us as adults, imagine what happens if we pass this on to our children?

It does not matter what a company calls its weight-loss approach; none have been shown through sound research to lead to long-term weight loss for more than a tiny fraction of those who use it. You might have noticed that many diet companies no longer use the word *diet*, they talk about "lifestyle" instead. But diets are still what they sell.

The multibillion-dollar diet industry has a huge advertising presence, and your daughter will see the ads everywhere. This decades-long marketing effort has convinced most people of a terrible fallacy—that fat people are fat because they lack the willpower to keep weight off over the long term. We are taught to shun fat people, to be fearful of becoming one of them, or, if we are already fat, to do all that we can to whittle our bodies down to a slimmer physique. The incredible thing is that after all this marketing and all the government campaigns, there is not a single country in the world that has successfully reduced obesity rates.

Healthy eating and regular exercise improve health, but do not necessarily lead to significant weight loss. It's more important, and more successful, to focus on being healthy.

The Way We Are Made

There's a reason why diets are not successful. Humans evolved for a tough Stone Age environment, when food was often scarce, and so our bodies are wired to protect our healthy weight. When we diet, our body thinks it's a famine and triggers mechanisms to try to put the weight back on. A study in the *New England Journal of Medicine* found the appetite-stimulating hormone, ghrelin, increased in dieters by approximately 20 percent. Appetite-suppressing hormones, such as leptin and peptide YY, were also found at unusually low levels. Our metabolic rate also slows if we diet—so that we can conserve weight!

Is the solution to just try, try again? Interestingly, research has found that over time dieting actually makes us fatter. A groundbreaking study by Dr. Dianne Neumark-Sztainer, of the University of Minnesota School of Public Health, showed adolescent girls who engage in weight-control behavior end up significantly heavier than their peers five years later. Another study tracked 15,000 participants aged between nine and fourteen. It found that preteens and teenagers who were put on diets were significantly more likely to gain weight than those who were not. And worst news of all—dieting is also the biggest predictor of an eating disorder, with one in five obese Australians now found to have eating disorder symptoms, despite maintaining a higher weight.

How Fat Shaming Just Makes Things Worse

Fat shaming is often used as a way to try to motivate us to achieve better health. Nothing could be worse. TV shows like *The Biggest Loser* humiliate their fat contestants while reinforcing the stereotype that all fat people are fat due to poor health choices. Yet research shows that being ashamed of one's weight was a risk factor for both those suffering from obesity and eating disorders, while also *reducing* the likelihood of a person engaging in regular physical activity. Given that exercise typically takes place in a public space, it makes sense that people—especially teenage girls who feel particularly ashamed of the way they look—would not feel comfortable wearing gym clothes or swimsuits or doing anything that draws attention to their bodies.

Bullying under the guise of health is fast becoming a national pastime. This hysteria toward fatness is killing us and our daughters. One study found obese children were 63 percent more likely to be bullied. While it's understandable that parents wish to help their child escape bullying, putting a child on a diet is not the solution. It makes them feel it's their fault.

School and other health programs tackling obesity the wrong way may cause great harm. Professor Jennifer O'Dea, of the University of Sydney, found "health education for child obesity prevention may result in . . . unplanned, undesirable and health-damaging effects such as starvation, vomiting, laxative abuse, diuretic and slimming abuse, and cigarette smoking to suppress appetite and as a substitute for eating." Eating Disorders Victoria (an Australian eating disorder support service) reports 8 percent of adolescent girls currently smoke to control their weight.

The Other Extreme

When we hear the words *eating disorder*, we most often think of people who are extremely thin. But, in fact, most eating-disorder sufferers are not emaciated, with those suffering from bulimia or binge-eating disorder often maintaining a "healthy weight" or higher. Anorexia—not eating to the point of serious weight loss—is certainly not helped by our obsession with weight and, in fact, many girls admire and idolize anorexic friends for their assumed iron will and self-control. Emerging research suggests anorexia is a brain disorder exacerbated by starvation. It takes intensive clinical help to overcome the disordered thinking and behavior, and without this there is a serious risk of damage or death.

Binge eating is a far more common problem. Eating large amounts of food in an intense burst is a natural response to dieting, as the body tries to hold on to fat stores. It turns up the appetite-stimulating hormones, and we become highly attuned to food, causing us to become obsessed and distracted with eating. Binge eating is our body's way of trying to help us survive. For reasons not fully understood, the anorexia sufferer's physiology does not "kick in" to help her survive; many anorexic patients report actually feeling better when they are starving themselves, and that's why it's such a dangerous condition.

What to Do Instead

Our bodies are constantly communicating to us: when we are hungry, we should eat; when we are approaching fullness, stop. Constipation is another signal that tells us we might have insufficient fiber in our diet. Our body has a biological system that internally regulates many facets of our survival—including blood pressure and body temperature, and strives to defend a set-point weight.

Dieting is a terrible trap. Many get caught in a vicious cycle of losing weight in the short term, only to experience a strong preoccupation with food and cravings that in turn leads to weight gain, so then they embark on a diet yet again. Numerous studies have shown weight cycling to be more detrimental to health than maintaining a higher but steady weight, so the idea that one should "try, try again" is actually a harmful one.

Many health professionals are now ditching weight as an appropriate measure of health and are instead embracing a health-centered approach known as Health at Every Size (HAES). HAES argues that fitness is actually a much more accurate assessment of health than size (except at statistical extremes). Body Mass Index (BMI) is a poor indicator of health. There are other biomarkers that can be used to measure health, such as blood pressure and heart rate. Two key principles are intuitive eating and finding physical movement that is joyful instead of focused on weight loss. Every day we should go to bed feeling good for having engaged in health-giving behavior rather than beating ourselves up for not yet being a certain number on the scales.

An Industry Out of Control

You may be shocked to learn that 95 percent of obesity research is funded by the weight-loss industry. No wonder our understanding of health and weight is so befuddled. The dieting industry is largely unregulated.

The food industry similarly needs tighter regulations. Why are toys sold with every Happy Meal, and high-sugar breakfast cereals marketed directly to children? If we want a healthier nation, environmental changes must take place, much like we saw with the tobacco industry losing its grasp as cigarettes were gradually banned from bars, advertising outlawed, and cigarettes lost their glamorous packaging. Blaming and shaming the individual will never achieve population health.

Australia recently developed a National Advisory Board for Body Image that has taken up a voluntary code of conduct to get the beauty and fashion industries to adopt healthier approaches. Unfortunately, the code was a flop. Chairperson of the advisory board Mia Freedman blogged, "NOTHING HAS CHANGED." *Dolly Magazine* was awarded the government's 2012 body image awards (the centerpiece of the board's initiatives) despite resurrecting a modeling competition for thirteen-year-old girls, sending the message that unless girls are hot, they're irrelevant. This was nothing short of an embarrassment. Other countries have begun making legislative changes. For example, Spain has looked into banning "cult of the body" advertisements that promote plastic surgery and dieting products until 10 p.m. each night. In 2008, France made it illegal for anyone—including magazines and advertisers—to incite "extreme thinness." In 2012, the Israeli government introduced a law banning the use of underweight models in magazines and on the catwalk.

While some continue to blame parents for their child's poor body image, an open letter signed by forty-five international health experts titled "The Impact of Media Images on Body Image and Behavior: A Summary of the Scientific Evidence" reported "overwhelming evidence" that media images contributed to body dissatisfaction and disordered eating. Another study reviewed seventy-seven studies involving 15,000 participants that showed media images had greater impact on young people today than in the 1990s. In other words, despite all the body-image initiatives, media images ultimately have more impact. Parents have some responsibility, though, and protective factors against disordered eating include helping children find physical activities they enjoy, modeling healthy behavior, having regular family meals, eating breakfast every day, and fostering healthy self-esteem and body image. Governments must take a more aggressive approach to industry if we really want to see a healthy world for our girls.

How You Can Help Your Daughter

1. Become the role model she needs. If you obsess about weight, so will she. Ditch the diet talk, don't watch those TV shows, and don't have fashion or weight-loss magazines around the house. Don't even think about going on a "diet."

2. Don't have soft drinks in the fridge. They confuse thirst with hunger, and even the diet brands have unhealthy chemicals in them. Have a jug of cold water.

3. Have meals together at a table, with no TV playing. When you watch TV while eating, you don't notice the food properly or really taste it. And you don't notice when you've had plenty. Noticing you are full happens a few minutes after you have eaten enough, so eating more slowly around the table allows everyone to notice when they are "full." At the table, only talk about positive things, make it a relaxed time, find out what has gone well in their lives; it's not a board meeting!

4. Don't get into "bad food, good food"; call it "everyday" food—the healthy things we eat all the time—and "sometimes food"—which we have occasionally for a treat. Eating "junk" food and feeling guilty about it just makes it worse. People binge then feel bad. Research shows that if you eat slowly and enjoy treat food, you actually don't eat as much of it. If you are ashamed, you wolf it down.

5. Be a family that moves. If Mom and daughter walk the dog or kick a ball around outside, or the whole family goes for a walk or to the park, a love of being physical will come naturally without it being "exercise."

Everything here applies just as much to boys!

Five Myths about Eating Disorders

Myth 1: People choose to have an eating disorder.

Fact: Eating disorders are *not* a choice, they are serious psychological illnesses that develop over time and have complex psychological bases.

Myth 2: You must be thin to have an eating disorder.

Fact: Most people who experience eating disorders are in fact in the "healthy weight range" or are even overweight.

Myth 3: Eating disorders only occur in females.

Fact: Eating disorders in males are rising, particularly in those under fourteen years (a quarter of eating disorder diagnoses in that age group are now males). Males are also more likely to "fly under the radar," given they are not expected to have eating disorders.

Myth 4: Anorexia is the only serious eating disorder.

Fact: Engagement in restricting food or weight-loss practices such as vomiting or laxative abuse renders any person vulnerable to serious medical complications. Further, experiencing any eating disorder is distressing and isolating for sufferers and thus they are susceptible to a significantly increased risk of self-harm and suicide.

Myth 5: People who develop eating disorders have been sexually abused.

Fact: Sexual abuse is a risk factor for developing many mental health conditions, including eating disorders. However, not everyone with an eating disorder has been sexually abused.

Finally, if your daughter does develop an eating disorder, you must remember that you are not to blame for the development of the illness; you are one of the best resources for her recovery. A comparable example is that a painkiller can help to remove a headache, but the headache is not caused by an absence of painkillers.

If your daughter does develop eating disorder symptoms, it is critical that you act on this immediately. Commencing treatment as soon as possible is vital because the illness can be avoided with early intervention; recovery outcomes will improve if treatment is commenced quickly. Ensure that you learn as much as possible about eating disorders so you can be a resource in recovery. Hold the hope for your daughter because a complete and total recovery is possible for everyone.

What Are Eating Disorders? How to Recognize
If Your Daughter Is at Risk

Eating disorders are patterns of behavior with food that are unhealthy or harmful if taken too far. Most people know of *anorexia*—a disorder within which people fail to eat enough food and run the risk of life-threatening weight loss. Thankfully, death from this disorder is still relatively rare, but it is dangerous and anorexics need immediate help. *Bulimia*—vomiting up one's food after eating in order to limit or reduce weight, is much more common. In practice, eating disorders are blurred, and there are many people of normal weight or above-average weight who eat in a disordered way. In all cases, though, there is danger and a need to get professional help and advice early—the sooner it's addressed, the better chances of recovery.

Early Warning Signs
A parent should start to worry about a possible eating disorder if they notice a cluster of changes in their daughter, including these:

* Weight fluctuations (whether the weight goes up or down).

* Change in mood, including becoming more anxious, angry, depressed, or withdrawn.

* Increased preoccupation with body shape or weight, such as increased weighing or "body checking."

* Changes in eating behavior, such as eliminating food groups or specific meals; eating becoming more regimented or ritualistic; or "regressed eating"—eating in a childlike way, for instance with special cups or child's crockery or cutlery.

* Increased distress around meal times or eating.

It is important to note that we are looking for a cluster of observable changes—any one of these behaviors alone could be due to another cause, such as an illness. Assessment and diagnosis of an eating disorder usually begins with checking that there is no physical basis for the symptoms. It's only when multiple changes are observed together that an eating disorder may be considered to be the likely cause.

Disordered Thinking

Along with the changes to eating behavior and mood, some unusual ways of thinking about food are evident in someone who is starting to have an eating disorder:

* Desire to maintain an unhealthily low body weight.

* An intense fear of weight gain or "becoming fat."

* A distorted perception about their appearance.

* A preoccupation with food prospectively (worrying about forthcoming meals or meal planning) and retrospectively (experiencing intense guilt or shame about food consumed).

* False beliefs around food or weight loss/management (such as eating dinner after 6 p.m. will result in excessive weight gain, or having four glasses of water before each meal will speed up the metabolism).

The Actual Behavior

Finally, the strongest clues to a disorder are actual eating behavior. You may notice:

* Intentional restriction of food; for example, eliminating meals like breakfast, eliminating entire food groups from the diet, or claims of a gluten or lactose or other new allergy.

* Bingeing, which is essentially consuming a large quantity of food in a short period of time, and eating with a sense of loss of control.

* Eating compulsively—feeling out of control while eating—or eating past fullness. (This can take place during normal meals and eating situations and can look relatively normal to a bystander, whereas bingeing is usually done in private and typically involves eating huge amounts of food.)

* Purging or "getting rid of" food through unhealthy compensatory behavior, such as vomiting, abusing laxatives, or excessive exercise.

Continued

The particular set of eating-disorder behavior exhibited will determine what diagnosis is made. It is normal for eating-disorder behavior to change over the course of the illness, and thus the diagnosis is also likely to change. In successful treatment, a person with an eating disorder may swing to the opposite behavior, and her therapist will help her to manage and work through this.

What to Do

If you are concerned that your daughter might have an eating disorder, it is vital that you act immediately. Early intervention is one of the best predictors of a complete recovery, and you should never wait until your daughter is "sick enough" to access help. Consult your family doctor or contact an eating-disorder nonprofit (see page 211) to arrange an assessment and find out the best way to access treatment in your area. Treatment for eating disorders is usually highly specialized, and it is best to start with "evidence-based treatment"—your GP or eating-disorder nonprofit will be able to advise on what this is in the case of your daughter.

The best predictor of success in treatment is the "therapeutic alliance"—finding a good fit between the therapist, your daughter, and yourself/your family. For individuals who don't respond to the first attempt of treatment, it is vital that further treatment be attempted. Ultimately, recovery tends to take place with the match of the right therapist, the right approach, and the right timing.

It is a good idea to read all you can about eating disorders, because this will assist you in being the best resource for your daughter's recovery.

It is very natural to feel worried, guilty, or even angry at a person with an eating disorder. This can sometimes get in the way of being helpful. For example, some parents blame the person with the eating disorder for getting sick because of the impact the eating disorder has on their marriage or on the family. This resentment can make it difficult for parents to do what is required to support a sick daughter in her recovery—assisting her to access treatment or just being supportive and kind to her and listening to her feelings.

CHAPTER TEN

Alcohol and Other Drugs

Paul Dillon lives in the inner city. He can tell you about the street price of amphetamines and what quality of ice is coming into the country right now. He knows what to do if someone has overdosed or drunk themselves into a coma. Paul is Australia's best-known drug educator and has been for years, working with schools and groups all over the country to make sure kids have a clear perspective and can keep themselves and their friends from dying in the name of a good time.

Indeed, Paul may well be responsible for the fact that since 2002, drug use and drinking among young people have actually gone down. He has some surprising insights and methods to help parents know when to relax and when to wake up in guiding their kids and themselves in a world of mind-altering chemicals, legal and illegal. When Paul visits a school, he shows some interesting slides. Most people are familiar with the graphs showing lots of kids using alcohol, less smoking, quite a few using cannabis, and so on down the list to ecstasy and heroin, but Paul simply turns this upside down. Depending a little on the country in which you are reading this, but pretty much consistently across the Western World, we have the following picture:

* Although many seventeen-year-olds have drunk alcohol, most do not drink to excess regularly, with some rarely touching the stuff. More than 25 percent of this age range say they are nondrinkers and almost 10 percent have never drunk alcohol at all.

* More than 70 percent of seventeen-year-old high school students have *never* smoked cannabis and probably won't.

* Ninety-seven percent of high school students have *never* used hallucinogens.

* Ninety-six percent have *never* used amphetamines. Of the 4 percent who have, most only tried them once or twice in the last year.

* Ditto for heroin or morphine.

* Cocaine is the same: 98 percent never use it and the 2 percent only used it once or twice.

* Ecstasy is a bit worse—only 92 percent have never used it (!) and of those who do, most are quite occasional users.

Paul gazes across the sea of young people sitting in school assembly halls and multipurpose rooms to watch his presentation, and when these slides come up he sees dozens of young people sit a little taller. They are the nondrinking, nondrugging kids suddenly realizing they are in the majority. This is really important for them, and you, to know about. Suddenly all that panic about kids getting wasted, and the pressure that this is what you are supposed to do to be cool starts to fade away.

In fact, not only are most kids of school age quite happy to avoid drugs and drinking, but (apart from a slight rise in the use of ecstasy) rates of drug usage and drinking has been falling, slowly but steadily, all through the 2000s. Today's young people are a bit over all that.

That's the good news, especially on drugs. In particular, Paul takes great pains to point out that drugs are a very minor problem for a small number of young people (for whom, of course, they are a big problem indeed). But he is not at all soft on harm reduction; alcohol, he says, is a different matter.

Alcohol products, which are legally produced and sold and heavily promoted (in fact, carefully designed) to appeal to young women, are destroying brains and causing huge risks to safety from accidents and violence. I've heard Paul come close to suggesting (and I am inclined to agree) that the alcohol industry probably encourages paranoia about drugs so that parents will be relatively relaxed that their daughters only use alcohol. More on the alcohol industry later.

For years, the folklore about alcohol is that a little bit won't hurt you, and that the "Mediterranean approach" of letting kids sip a little wine at mealtimes helps to make them sensible drinkers and takes away the rebellion in drinking. A book by a leading girls' schools organization actually advised this just last year.

It's a nice theory, but it's recently been proven totally wrong. Having small amounts of alcohol in childhood or the early teens to midteens is now known to change the brain in startling ways, making it more vulnerable to alcohol and alcoholism afterward. Kids shouldn't be allowed anywhere near it.

In fact, the brain effects of even modest amounts of drinking support the strong argument for adopting the US age limit of twenty-one, which works fine. The fake license issues tend to take place at around the age of nineteen in the US, whereas for Australians, it's more like sixteen. That's three or four years of better brain protection.

And although Paul's upside-down graphs make a good point, alcohol usage is still concerning, even limited to a minority group. Around one in seventeen young people drink at dangerous levels every week. For women (whose bodies are smaller and have a different chemistry), the level of dangerous drinking is consuming more than four standard drinks in one episode, while for girls who don't yet have a developed liver (which doesn't happen until around the age of twenty-one!), it should be much less than that. Six percent of girls who are still at school drink at levels that are dangerous for fully grown women at least once a week.

The newest concern, which few parents or girls have yet absorbed, is that alcohol is a risk factor for breast cancer, accounting for about a third of all breast cancers. (While breast cancer has a genetic component, it is almost always caused by environmental toxins of some kind or other. Flooding your bloodstream with ethanol is not good for soft tissues.)

This, then, is the picture that we described in our mental health overview earlier. Most girls are fine, but the group that are not fine are in real trouble.

So far we've been looking at kids still at school. One of the wonderful things about school is that it has a huge, protective, mental health benefit. For most kids, schools are still friendly places with routine and structure, where there are adults who care about you and friends on tap with a wide range of ideas and attitudes.

When kids leave school, all the mental health indicators—suicide rates, self-harm, drinking and drugs, depression and anxiety—leap upward. It's lonely out in the big world.

What Parents of Girls Should Know and Teach

The use of drugs by girls is not correlated to any of the things you might think. It's not connected to income—rich girls and poor girls are at equal risk. It's not related to educational level. It's not connected to intelligence or ability. Only one factor stands out as a reliable predictor: parental supervision or monitoring. Parents who know where their kids are, know what they are doing, and are around and in their life, tend not to have kids who drink or use drugs. And if things do occasionally go haywire, they care and they get involved to make sure it doesn't happen again.

This involvement isn't "guard the door" suspicion, but caring conversations, firmness around where you are and with whom, and friendly but clear negotiations about proving you are able to stay safe and careful.

All the adolescent experts I spoke to in writing this book were very critical (that's the polite word) of a certain kind of parent who wants to be their child's friend—the mom who buys the drinks, the dad who gives his daughter fifty dollars when she heads into the city to party with her friends. ("Party" used to be a word for friends who loved each other, hosting everyone at their home for delicious food, drinks, conversation, and dancing. Now it just means getting smashed. It's done in anonymous clubs and bars where you can't hear yourself speak. That's intentional—if kids start talking, they don't drink as much. The owners want them hot, restless, and revved, because that sells more drinks.)

Around 35 percent of all the alcohol drunk by kids of school age (and therefore illegal drinkers) is provided by parents. But then, at least, it's not drugs!

One particular drug is almost exclusively the choice at "parties" (that is, clubs) and that is ecstasy. Ecstasy makes you feel energetic and loving. It releases a weeks' supply of endorphins from your body (which is why you feel crap for a week afterward). The problem is that it's usually made in a some basement by someone called Slug who doesn't always know, or care, what goes into it. Nobody knows what they are taking. This is the thing to quietly, and calmly, explain to your teenager. This stuff doesn't come from Switzerland.

It's possible we are making our kids too trusting of pills overall. We prescribe them to an awful lot of little boys who just need more chance to run around. And when a child has a headache, we reach for the Tylenol. Paul points out that 90 percent of adolescent headaches are caused by dehydration, and a nice glass of water might be more help.

The Alcohol Pushers

Several years ago, the alcohol industry was worried because drinking levels were steady or falling. Their best customers had died young. The companies needed a new market, because in industry, growth is everything. Their researchers talked to teenage girls. (In the US, they pay schools $500 and get access to school kids for all kinds of research into how better to harm them.) It turned out that girls don't like the taste of spirits. This was a tragic waste of a good market, and so the industry devised alcopops—fizzy and sugary drinks that tasted like juice but were loaded with rum, brandy, vodka or gin. And, whoopee, girls began to drink them by the caseload.

In Australia, the government, under pressure from health groups, attempted to raise the tax on these drinks. The industry created a storm, and a compromise was reached (lobbyists don't just vote like the rest of us, they exert other forms of influence). Alcopop consumption fell, though not enough. Girls also got used to spirits. Today, to preempt the cost of drinks in clubs, you can see girls on trains into the city slugging supermarket liquor so they can arrive smashed.

Wherever you are reading this, you can test your politicians' integrity. Ask them to tax alcohol heavily, especially those products favored by young people or designed to entice them. Young drinkers are very price sensitive, a 20 percent price rise often deals them out. Get them to ban all advertising of alcohol aimed at the young—it can survive as an honest industry providing a valuable product, it just won't be a cash cow that costs us all in hospitals and road crashes. If they don't, individually or as a party, support these changes, then you know who owns them, and it's not the voters.

Binge Drinking

So despite the good news of the big picture, a small but sizeable cohort of girls and young women are drinking enough for the rest of us. These girls drink so much, one or more nights a week, that their bodies are permanently being changed. Teenagers do not have fully grown kidneys; they cannot absorb or process the alcohol from their bloodstreams anywhere near as fast. Serious harm occurs to their growing brain, and they are 60 percent more likely to have an alcohol problem as an adult.

Binge drinking by girls and young women has swept the world, even reaching countries where alcohol hasn't been a problem in the past—such as France or Italy. The boys can't believe their luck; the sexual availability of these girls has soared.

The reason for the upswing in girls drinking at dangerous levels is a combination of factors. Venues for entertainment and socializing are heavily alcohol focused. There is a massive marketing effort to make drinking look adult and cool. The pressure to conform and just drink to fit in is enormous. But there seems to be something else, too, a kind of desperate wish to get wasted, a kind of temporary suicide, to knock reality out with an almost self-destructive zeal. All the pressures we have listed through this book add up, and for some girls it comes out in drinking, for others in cutting, others in disordered eating, others in random sex. Sometimes, it's all of the above. These girls need help.

What to Do?

If you are a parent, love your daughter. Do all the things in this book from the time she is small. If she starts problem drinking anyway, get help. Alcoholism is a metabolic condition in some people and just has to be managed.

Don't give drinks to underage kids. Don't drink more than the odd glass yourself if you don't need to, or only on special occasions and moderately. Especially try not to drink when you are stressed, so that she sees you "needing" alcohol or, worse, affected by it. That's role modeling of the worst kind.

Don't let her simply go out into the city to cruise clubs until she is old enough to take care of herself. Depending on where you live, that could be twenty-one. Have a definite deal about getting home, and a rescue arrangement that you will go get her *anywhere anytime* when needed.

The aim is for your daughter to be able to go out, have a good time, and not be harmed. You are on the same side as her, just more aware of the big picture. While she is under twenty-one, her life is your responsibility. But even when she is older and still living under your roof, you have an opportunity to intervene, in a friendly and concerned way, to keep her safe. Even a caring roommate would do that. Being home at an agreed time and not coming back drunk are reasonable requirements in any household where people care about each other.

Esther's Law

Esther, who helps manage my teacher seminars, is barely twenty-five, and a warm and idealistic member of Generation Y. I asked her how her friends dealt with partying. Simple, she said, we have the Voice of Reason. She and her friends realized they needed someone, rather like the designated driver, who stayed straight and could decide whether it was time to go home, if that street was a good place to walk, and any other decisions about people and places that would keep them out of harm. Each night they went out together, in a group of five or six, they would vote for who would be the Voice of Reason. That person would only have one drink. And the pact was that what she says, we all do, without even a moan of complaint.

I asked whether this was an onerous task, suspecting for some reason that it might fall to her more often than not. No, she assured me, it's an honor: "Some of the girls we would *never* choose. We do rotate it a little, but three or four of us kind of take it seriously that we love each other, and we get everyone home safe. We're proud of it."

CHAPTER ELEVEN

Girls and the Online World

by Melinda Tankard Reist

At conferences of parents and teachers around the country, I have often spoken alongside the wonderful feminist and girls' advocate, Melinda Tankard Reist. If I arrive late, I know how to find the theater, because the sound of a thousand people gasping or saying, "Oh no!" in unison is hard to miss. Melinda's PowerPoint presentation of what young people will encounter online leaves audiences reeling, and she is very restrained in what she chooses to show. As parents, we need to know about this. A multibillion-dollar industry—larger than sport, larger than Hollywood— now exists to sell porn, and young people are its main target. And even useful tools like Facebook can be horribly misused if parents aren't there to help. Melinda writes about all this with unequaled clarity.

I'm a writer, speaker, and commentator. I have four children. Like almost everyone I know, the Internet is a huge part of my life.

Today I've been trying to write a chapter for this book. So this is what I did instead. I checked my two Facebook pages. I posted some articles on them, along with thanks to those who had sent supportive messages. I shared a couple of petitions and asked people to vote. I tweeted links to articles and blogs, replied to tweets, and re-tweeted other people's tweets. I tried to reply to emails, gave up, and watched a couple of YouTube clips—including one of my son playing a cover of Daft Punk's "Digital Love" (you should hear it, it's great!). I stared dreamily at online photos of the beach where I'll be vacationing soon. I contacted my kids through Facebook (the guitarist and outdoor-adventurer daughter who lives out-of-state, not the two younger ones who live at home, although I have been known to message the sixteen-year-old to get her attention).

Having eaten up hours in this frenzy of virtual activity, I've now had to shut it all down to start doing my homework.

New forms of social media have provided opportunities for my work, while bringing with them new problems. Like distraction! The difficulty of processing thousands of messages. Lots of things I could get distressed or worried about. And I'm an adult. I know that I need to balance out the hours I spend in online darkness as part of my research with good things that lift me up. I know when to walk away.

Trading Human Contact for Friends You've Never Met

But what about our teen and tween girls, who live out their lives on social media and who can't log off because they are afraid they'll miss something? Who are constantly texting, updating their Facebook pages, sending Instagrams on their smartphones, and seeking the thrill of instant gratification from responses received in seconds? Some girls sleep with their phones beside them, every beep alerting them through the night to a tweet or a post.

As a young woman writing in *The Times* admitted, "I consistently trade actual human contact for the more reliable high of smiles on MySpace, winks on Match.com, and pokes on Facebook."

What of the girls who are anxious about not having enough "friends" on Facebook—or worse, suffer the blow of being unfriended? It's a whole new source of anxiety—negative responses to their posts, or what might happen if they don't check for a while and someone has said something nasty?

All Is Revealed

Of course there are many benefits of social media. It facilitates communication and bonding. It can bring friends together. Girls can explore their creativity online—posting artwork, fashion design, their poetry, and writing. They can join causes that they care about.

But often, in this new world, everything is revealed—there is little holding back, from mundane updates to outpourings of grief and despair. As she creates her digital self-portrait, this all-day everyday marketing of herself, her online footprint is indelible. Privacy is often a distant consideration.

Christine Rosen, writing in *The New Atlantis,* called it "the timeless human desire for attention that emerges as the dominant theme of these vast virtual galleries."

Tell Me I'm Pretty

My colleagues and I are concerned about the girls who don't feel good about themselves, who so often look for approval from others. Social networking sites invite them to ask not just a few friends if they think they are okay, but the whole world.

In 2012, girls as young as eleven began posting clips on YouTube asking the world to judge them by answering one simple question: "Am I ugly or pretty?" There are now hundreds of "Ugly/Pretty" videos in this twenty-first century remake of "Mirror, mirror on the wall."

These poignant postings, viewed by millions, had girls like Kendal saying, "A lot of people tell me I'm ugly. I think I'm ugly and fat." The fifteen-year-old attracted 4,000,000 views and 107,000 anonymous responses. One of them: "Y do you live, and kids in Africa die?" And another: "You need a hug . . . around your neck . . . with a rope . . . ."

Vulnerable teens and tweens invite scrutiny and judgment from a cyberworld renowned for cruelty, bullying, and pack attacks. When what comes back is a torrent of abuse, the girls appear nonchalant, shrugging it off with quizzical half-smiles, like it really didn't matter that much, when you know it did.

In the online environment, comments are magnified. A girl's fragile sense of self can be smashed instantly by rumor spreading and gossip. This can act as a trigger to self-harm, suicidal thoughts, and suicide.

Online bullying—experienced by at least 10 percent of young people in Australia (see chapter 8)—can lead to death. Melbourne mother Karen Rae has no doubt that cyberbullying was responsible for the death of her fourteen-year-old daughter. She told the media: "Friday night she was on the Internet and told me about some message that had come through, and she wanted to die because of the message."

Rewarding Exhibitionism

In 2012, a craze took off called Naked Selfies, in which people post images of themselves naked. But the sites also show thousands of images of young women that have clearly not been taken by themselves—they may not even know they've been posted.

Teenage girls have written to me asking that I share their stories of being made drunk at parties, being taken advantage of sexually, and their images being uploaded on Facebook while they're still at the party. It is girls like these who pay the price in being shamed and disgraced, not those who take and upload the images.

There are numerous "slut" pages where men (often punishing their exes) post images of women they deem to fit the title. Pictures I saw included a woman with a black eye and a young girl in a backyard in a dress, looking relaxed and happy. It seems any female can be given this title.

Rape-joke pages abound—you couldn't even count them. These contribute to how we are raising boys to accept a callous and brutal version of masculinity, indifferent to suffering.

Growing Up in a Pornified World

This is the first whole generation of children to grow up so exposed to pornography. In Australia, 53 percent of girls under thirteen now report that they have seen porn. It's 97 percent by the age of sixteen. Some parents have said to me, "My child wouldn't go looking for porn." But your child doesn't have to be "looking"—it will find them. Facebook is covered in it. So is Google Images. Pornographers have deliberately created sites based on popular children's cartoon characters such as Dora the Explorer. Girls often stumble on porn while doing their homework, typing an innocuous word into a search engine. Or boys at school show it to them on their phones.

It's an unprecedented assault on the sexual development of young people, which shapes their behavior. This is the first generation to grow up seeing sexual violence before having sex—often even before they've had their first kiss. Studies of boys who have seen porn show they are more likely to accept the idea that it's okay to force a girl to have sex.

Young people look to porn for sex education, but it is a poor handbook, a distortion of respect-based sexuality, stripped of intimacy and connection. It tells girls they are mere service stations for men and boys. Boys are acting out the scripts they learn from porn. Even if a girl doesn't like what's happening, she's often confused because porn tells her she should enjoy it.

There's no doubting porn's influence on the popular practice of sexting. Even ten-year-olds are sending sexual images of themselves through phones. Girls can be vulnerable to being made into "amateur" online pornography. Social media (such as chat sites) makes it easier to recruit young women into the industry.

Tweens and teens are also encouraged to reveal themselves on webcams. It's tempting to post sexy and glam photos online when all their friends are doing it, and to get lots of comments. If a girl hasn't been praised and valued for other things, this may be the one place where she attracts compliments and rewards. But she may not know or understand where these images might end up, or that they are out there forever.

In July 2007, MySpace expelled 29,000 registered sex offenders who had signed up for memberships using their real names. The ones with false names are probably still there. Warn children that the girl or boy they are talking to may be a man, and that they must never share details with strangers about where they live, their phone number, and never ever arrange to meet.

In alerting parents to these trends, I want to make clear that my concerns have nothing to do with shaming girls for their sexuality. Rather, this is about naming a culture that teaches them that their sexuality is all that they are and that sells ideas of sexuality back to them in distorted and harmful ways.

Encouraged to Harm

Websites that promote self-harming behavior are a significant danger to girls. Tumblr and LiveJournal have thousands of pages dedicated to anorexia and bulimia, self-harm, and suicide. These sites are filled with angst, body hatred, messages of self-loathing, images of women jumping out of windows or dead in baths, arms crisscrossed with cutting scars.

The "pro-ana" and "pro-mia" sites promote anorexia and bulimia as a lifestyle choice, not an illness. If your daughter visits these sites for "starvation tips of the day," she has a serious problem—or soon will have.

Harriet Brown, author of *Brave Girl Eating: A Family's Struggle with Anorexia*, has called for such sites to be shut down:

If I could shut down every thinspo Tumblr and blog site, I'd do it in a heartbeat. I'd do it without giving the First Amendment another thought. Because there's nothing free or authentic about what's being expressed. Thinspo is not self-expression because it's not these young women's true selves that invite emaciation and worship at the altar of jutting hipbones. The longing for extreme thinness, for the self-annihilation of starvation, is not rational. It's not a choice. . . .

Every one of them is locked in a prison she can't get out of, in the grip of an illness that can't be reasoned with or rationalized. In their postings . . . they're crying out for help.

Rebekah McAlindon is a nineteen-year-old student in recovery from eating disorders who wrote on my blog: "As a young woman in recovery, seeing others succumb to such behavior is triggering, distressing, and saddening." Her advice is:

If you are a parent, please, please monitor your child's Internet history. If you are in recovery from an eating disorder, and struggle to avoid opening these types of websites, let someone know. Perhaps ask a friend to block them for you. If you're courageous enough, block them yourself . . .

If we can all support each other in this endeavor and choose to steer clear of proanorexic and probulimic sites, perhaps it will be one small but significant change to reducing the prevalence of eating disorders—and the terrible harm and suffering they cause.

Following the suicide of a sixteen-year-old Melbourne girl in 2012, her mother told ABC Television she had no idea of her daughter's online life—one full of negativity and encouragement to self-harm. Paige McIntyre was sharing her self-hating thoughts and photos of self-harm on Facebook, but her family didn't know about her secret life. When Paige took her life, thousands of messages were posted on her Facebook page. And the calls and texts kept coming, until her mother texted back, requesting they stop. "There's no 3G in heaven," she told them.

The Internet alone won't kill a girl, but it can easily worsen existing vulnerability.

Help direct your daughter away from sites worshipping death and telling them how to achieve it. There are positive, helpful, and professionally created websites to help girls to deal with depression or self-doubt.

While lots of Paige's friends—she had three hundred on Facebook—were sympathetic and caring, the time she spent "with" them was ultimately spent alone in her room many hours every night. The loving contact and close personal care she so craved could not be found in that space. Her mother says she felt cut off from her daughter, who was absorbed in her online life. But in a girl so vulnerable, it's face-to-face care, deep understanding, and adult rather than just peer-group focus that is needed through those very painful times.

Even if your daughter only uses the Internet in safe ways, be aware that she can still spend too much time online. There is a concern in mental-health circles that social media can limit or narrow girls' lives. It can encourage narcissistic (obsessively self-focused) behavior at a time when girls should be encouraged to think beyond themselves, to become whole, well-rounded citizens out in the real world. Girls have been imprisoned in narrow worlds too much in the past—we don't want to see it happening all over again.

Educate your daughter to be independent, to think of herself as valuable because of who she is, not because of what other people think of her. In the end, this will be her strongest armor.

What Can Parents Do?

By now, you're probably thinking of smashing the home computers, removing all mobile phones from your kids, and tossing the iPads out the window. Those feelings are understandable. But there are things we can do to help our children navigate online spaces and to interact online in ways that are positive and respectful.

* Show a positive interest in the technology your child is using. If you don't have your own account, create one, and explore the privacy options. Make sure your child is using the maximum privacy settings. Some parents make it a condition that, for a child to have an account on social media, she must have you as a friend. However, be aware that being a "friend" of your child on Facebook does not guarantee that you'll see everything she shares. Many young people have worked out how to block certain people (Mom and Dad) from seeing individual posts. This will be a challenge, which is why it is important to keep the lines of communication regarding safety and boundaries open.

* Know the rules. Your kids are not supposed to have a Facebook account until they are thirteen. They may feel left out, but if we parents get firmer on this, we will help each other with the job we have to do. Talk to your friends and get them to do the same.

* Have filtering devices installed, and place the computer in a public place in the home. ISPs are not yet required to filter at the source; we have to do what we can on the home front.

* Set limits on the time allowed for social networking. It isn't very life enhancing to have it operating 24/7. It's especially important for good sleep (see chapter 6) to have screen-free time before going to bed.

* Keep the channels of communication open so that if kids see something online that distresses them, they won't be ashamed to tell you about it. If you suspect your daughter is visiting sites that are harmful, raise the issue with her: intervene.

* Above all, try to stay connected to your daughter. Strong connections with parents reduce the chance of risky teenage behavior.

* Know the law. If harassment or threats to injure or kill occur over the phone or the Internet, the senders are at risk of criminal charges. The same is true if an eighteen-plus-year-old posts sexualized images of younger people.

* Get active on the big picture: campaign for radical cultural change to address sexualization, objectification, and pornification (see Author's Notes). Experts worldwide believe we have created a toxic media culture, and we now need to clean it up—to create a more caring, respectful, and child-friendly place for them to grow up in.

PART THREE

Girls and Their Parents

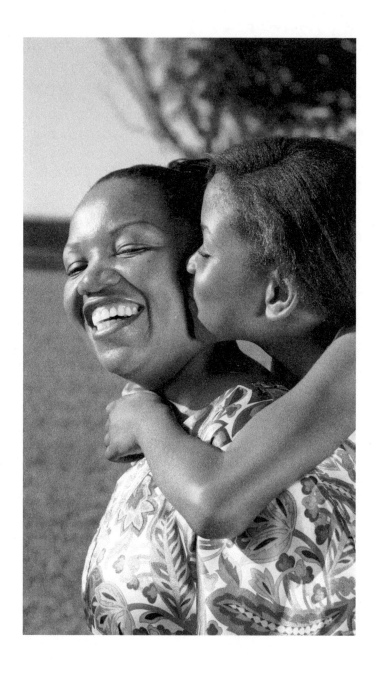

CHAPTER TWELVE

Girls and Their Moms

There's one fact about raising a girl that nobody disagrees with, and that is the centrality of mothers. The reason for this is simple: a mother is the role model, the person of the same gender who has the most effect, from the earliest time, for 95 percent of girls. A stay-at-home dad could be the main caregiver and have a huge effect; a substitute aunt or grandmother might step in for a mom who can't be there, but, for most girls, Mom is the person who teaches them what it means to be a woman. That's an awesome thing.

A girl might at different times adore her mom or hate her, admire her or criticize her—usually, in the twenty years of growing up, they will do all of the above!—but however it goes, no daughter ever says her mother wasn't hugely important. Long after you are gone, your daughter will remember your smile and your touch, what you taught her, and how you made her feel. She will pass all this on in the way she loves her children, and that love will go on down the generations.

How Role Modeling Works

When you think about it, what children have to learn while growing up is incredibly complex. It's not just things like riding a bike or ballet—everything we do has to be learned. How to be patient, how to give orders, how to argue with a husband amicably so he really gets what you are saying, how to use humor to keep spirits up when exhausted, how to love—these are not things you can learn from books. We learn to be human from watching other humans. Without role models, we would be clueless, and our lives impossibly hard. People without good role models often end up in trouble or in jail. (Support workers for "mothers at risk" often find that they have simply never seen someone discipline a child kindly, only pinch them, lock them in a closet, or slap them on the face. They literally did not know there was another way.)

The brains of children are wired to watch and copy. Special networks of nerves called *mirror neurons* link our eyes and our muscles, so we observe what others do and take that into our own behavior without even knowing it. You will notice you have mannerisms that your mother or father had. That's your mirror neurons at work. This

Being a Stepmom

One-third of all moms today are stepmoms. Stepmothering a daughter is a generous and beautiful act, because the love and closeness has to grow from scratch. Stepmothers tell me that the secret is in not forcing oneself on a daughter who didn't choose you and may have powerful feelings of both loyalty and loss toward her biological mom. Don't aim to replace her, but to grow a new relationship alongside her. Trust and intimacy take time—stepchildren have to come to you, on an emotional level. Be calm, be kind, and love will grow.

Throughout history, millions of kids have found additional or different mothers from the ones they were born to. Nobody needs to get less. A girl needs lots of love, and the more role models in her life, the better off she is.

is why each child becomes like the people they grow up around. Musicians create musicians, gardeners or animal lovers create a new generation of the same. If your kids love you, they will want to be like you.

So, brace yourself—you know where this is going, don't you? Your daughter is going to turn into you—plus whatever other role models or extra ingredients she can add to improve on the basic model! She will carry you inside her. If you can be your best self as a mother, then she will get the best start—she will take in the very best you have to give.

Cleaning Up Your Act

So let's get practical. What are the ways in which your role modeling might lead her to get a good or a bad start? Cast a quick glance over your life.

* Are you able to get along with men, or is that a disaster area in your life?
* Do you know how to make and keep good friends?
* Do you know how to relax?
* Do you know how to keep your promises?
* Do you know how to keep going when the road is hard and long?

She can learn these things from you.

There are other, more everyday things we show our daughters inadvertently. Stress is a big one. In my talk called "Secrets of Happy Children," I tell parents a rather stunning thing: your children cannot be more relaxed than *you*. That's because, at least in the early years, their level of stress rises and falls on the levels of their mom's and dad's and anyone else nearby. They are like a cork bobbing about on the waves of their mom's and dad's stress levels. Even newborn babies know about this. I once worked with a family in therapy who brought their baby along in a bassinet. The baby would vomit every time they got to a certain difficult topic. The rest of the hour, it was peaceful—but very alert!

Stress may seem difficult to control, but with help you can learn how to calm your body even in tough situations. Pregnancy is a great time to start a yoga relaxation or a meditation class. It's easiest to learn from someone you like (your mirror neurons will help you). A tape or DVD is next best (a book is helpful, but you will have to really be determined).

Every day you can choose how stressful you want your life to be, and what your daughter will observe and learn from you. The way you drive is a classic example. If you yell at other drivers, curse them for going slowly, drive up close behind them, make racist comments, or even just tap your fingers anxiously on the wheel, your daughter sees that. Sometimes we have no idea how dangerous our children perceive our driving to be. My daughter told her mom that she didn't want to drive with me. My driving style is not fast, it's actually way too relaxed. I leave it to the last minute to change lanes, do creative U-turns, and depend on my amazing ability to back into parking spots. It was scaring her witless. I had to develop a whole new approach to driving, because I really wanted her to feel safe with me.

Girls watch their moms (and dads) for the way they treat other people—if they are kind to others, if they volunteer for things, belong to community groups, stop and help someone who looks lost or distressed on the sidewalk.

Having kids means keeping a check on our emotions. They are often really frightened by unexplained intensity. We need to moderate ourselves, because they are little and vulnerable, something we easily forget. We can have and show our feelings, but not be overwhelmed by them.

Each gender has risk factors—in boys, it can be arrogance. With daughters, though, we have to guard against setting an example of martyrdom. A *martyr* is someone who doesn't put their own needs into the equation. Our girls need to see us taking a healthy interest in our own activities, our own health, our own creative time, our own spirit. Otherwise, how will they ever learn to do the same?

Maximizing Your Example

You can magnify your role modeling in one simple way: by explaining why you do things. Girls listen to what we say, even before they can speak. By explaining our choices and actions, they get a mental map of why people act the way they do. People who act badly often do so because they are not thinking much, they simply react emotionally to everything that comes along. People who act well have usually figured out some guidelines for living, and that helps them choose. So share your reasons with your daughter. One example might be striving to understand the motives of others: "That person is speeding, but perhaps it's an emergency, or they are having a bad day. Hope they'll be okay."

An important thing to teach your kids is that there is long term and short term. Finishing your schoolwork is hard when you would rather be swimming or playing computer games, but it's better to finish it so you can really relax. By high school, the idea can be absorbed that if you want a job that is fun, pays well, and where other people don't boss you around, you need some qualifications. So it's worth putting in a bit of effort and passing everything in high school. And so on.

Explain your values to your kids: that it's good to take care of yourself, but also to be caring for others, that it really helps if people keep their agreements, that most situations can be solved with some compromise, that everyone's voice counts, that honesty is better in the long run. They might roll their eyes, but you will see them adopting your philosophy a day or two later, or with their friends when you aren't even around.

So ask yourself, what are the core beliefs that you live your life by? Be sure to let your daughter know.

Letting Go

If all goes well, mothers and daughters end up being lifelong friends. However, in the late teen years, some distance is necessary if they are to grow and become themselves. Also, they need to have other role models in their life. Recognizing this means we can avoid clinging to them and taking this distancing personally. It can be hard, but our kids do need space. Micky Foss, a mother in northern New South Wales, Australia, told me this story:

My best friend's seventeen-year-old daughter stays with us overnight once a week.

The other morning when she left for school, I went with her to the front door, helped her with some of her things, kissed her goodbye, and wished her a good day. She said, in a jubilant and excited voice, "Oh, you are so sweet! You take me to the door, help me, and kiss me good-bye. My mother would never do that. She just calls 'Bye' from inside the house, and then I leave. I wish she would kiss me good-bye."

I went inside and mused over that for a while. The fact of the matter is that my friend's daughter is my "substitute" daughter. I would love to accompany my own sixteen-year-old girl to the door, kiss her good-bye, and with all my heart wish her a good day. However, she would hate that.

I surmised from this that, no matter what mothers do with their teenage daughters, the daughters appear to want the opposite—that is, whatever they don't get or have.

Why? From how I see it, this is part of the natural separation process. My daughter would think I was "babying" her. She would think I thought her incapable of getting herself out the door, and she would not want my kisses. I used to do all that, and she used to lap it up. Not anymore! She has to develop and form herself as an individual without her mother (me) doing what I did when she was little. And although I have known my friend's daughter since she was a baby, I am not her mother, so she has no need or desire to separate from me. She can, without any emotional dilemmas, enjoy my care and love for her.

I told my friend how her daughter responded to me. My friend will now take her daughter to the door in the morning and kiss her good-bye.

My bet is that, within a week, her daughter will push her away and say,
"Leave me be! How old do you think I am?"
Time will tell.

Home as a Haven

Something I have learned from great parents is worth passing on. It's good to look at the whole vibe in your house—the emotional atmosphere that you as parents create for everyone to live in.

The big world outside is stressful. Schools are often way too big and anonymous; the school day is hurried, nerves get jangled and frayed. Often our towns are grimy, and strangers who don't care much about us are all around. Some kids even have to deal with hostility or violence. There is very little natural space in our lives to be quiet with nature, the wind and sky or water. Because of all this, the need for home to be peaceful and safe is essential—especially for girls, whose senses are fine-tuned to the nuances of sensory inputs all around them.

So it really helps that home is a calm place. It doesn't mean that you don't have some fun TV on straight after school for half an hour to chill out, or some music, but notice the "temperature"—is it peaceful or jangling? Do you welcome the children home, give them some food and drink, and encourage them to unwind, or pile on some demands and rush about yourself?

Routine and structure soothes children, they know what is what, and can be more free and creative because they don't have to be hypervigilant.

Here are some other things that help:

* Shared meals at fixed times, where everyone sits at a table and there is no TV, really helps (there is even research to show this).

* Set bedtimes and set times to get ready for bed, and for activities that lead to bedtime—like baths or showers, story reading, or reading time for leisure before they fall asleep.

* An electronic blackout around bedtime; phones should be left on their chargers in the kitchen, not under the pillow to bother them with playground politics late into the night.

* Seasonal rituals that are exciting, with an enlarged family circle and the buzz of being in a large group where they still belong and matter.

* Silly games like Pictionary or family concerts and talent quests among the extended family to help people be playful across all generations.

* Great celebrations of birthdays—not expensive, but with time and effort and some care to make it something the kids really remember.

* One-to-one time, with just Mom, or just Dad, and daughter, such as a weekend away once a term, just the two of you, where you sleep, cook, do activities, and speak with nobody else—no partner, no other siblings—so she can actually feel your 100 percent care for her and store this in her memory banks.

* Visits and sleepovers with favorite aunts or grandparents, again to have that one-to-one opportunity.

* Family holidays where everyone can chill out—avoid expensive resorts where some bored young adults run "Kidz Clubs," and parents don't get any closer to their children than they do during the rest of the year. Often holidays are the times children remember as the most special in their lives, because they saw their parents actually relaxed and happy and glad to be with them.

* An annual cleanup of unwanted clothes, books, and toys, perhaps at the start of the new school year, to make their rooms spacious, clean, and "new"—and to give stuff to where it can help someone else.

This has been a broad sweep of ideas, and I hope some of them have captured your imagination.

Motherhood carries some natural grief: your children are headed out into the big world, and the better you raise them, the further they may go. But, despite the distance, kids raised with love grow closer and closer to their mothers. Your place in their hearts will always be as if you were standing right beside them.

A Great Film about Mothers

You might have heard of a movie called *Spanglish*, with Adam Sandler and Paz Vega in the lead roles. Often mistaken for a comedy and overlooked, this wonderful film about a Mexican mother and daughter coming to live with a wealthy American family tells a powerful story about mothering girls. The values of the two cultures are sharply in contrast: in one, possessions, fashion, and shopping are how love is shown, and this puts deep-down pressure on everyone. In the other, loyalty, effort, and being true to yourself are what matters most.

In the opening sequences, the American mother buys her daughter clothes one size too small to "motivate" her to lose weight. The daughter's excitement at seeing the clothes turns to bitter disappointment, and the scene is set for some real learning.

The Mexican daughter and the American daughter are touching to watch as they struggle with growing up. The contrast between how daughters are raised in each culture is very enlightening. The movie ends with an unforgettable quote from the Mexican daughter, some years later as she looks back on her childhood. She is writing an application for a college scholarship, which asks about who she is: "If I get accepted to this college I will be thrilled, but it won't define me. My sense of who I am comes powerfully and happily from one single fact—that I am my mother's daughter."

Imagine if your daughter is able to say that when she is a woman, grown up, independent, and strong. What would it take, for that to be so? Wouldn't that be worth a whole lot of time and care? Wouldn't that just be amazing?

In a Nutshell

* For better or worse, moms are the most powerful influence in a girl's life. This is because you role-model a very strong example of how to be a female human being.

* Just knowing this can cause you to reexamine a lot of the things you do.

* Especially important is how you role-model relating to others— including her father. How you drive a car, how you speak about others—everything you do becomes part of her.

* A big issue is the stress level you create in the home and in your life. You can literally set the stress levels in your daughter's body by how you set your own.

* Letting go is part of helping her grow up. From the age of sixteen, she may at times want you not to crowd her too much. This doesn't mean you don't stay in charge, though.

* Get it right with your daughter, get to know her at a deep level, and it will be a lifelong joy to you both.

CHAPTER THIRTEEN

Girls and Their Dads

They pause at the top of the stairs, the father and his little girl. She peers down the long flight of steps, and frowns a little. Then, without even looking beside her, she reaches for his hand, and it's there, and she grasps it. Now she steps out boldly down the first step, and the second, as he does the same beside her. She is singing to herself in rhythm as they descend. And he feels pretty good, too.

Fathers, to their young daughters, seem to be almost magical beings. They often go away to strange places and come back each day. Their voices are booming, deep, and loud. They smell funny, but mostly in a good way. Often they represent fun, excitement, and a stirring up of the daily routine. All being well, they make Mommy smile. Girls of all ages deeply want to love their dads and be loved back by them.

In recent decades, we've woken up to the value and importance of dads. (As late as the 1970s in Australia, if a mother died and there was no other family, the children would automatically have been put in an orphanage, the father would not have even been given the chance to try to raise them. How shattering that double grief must have been to thousands of dads and their children.)

Today we know that dads feel as deeply, can care as well, and are as vitally important as moms. (And a mom and dad who work as a team are pure gold.) Girls with an involved dad have been found in many studies to have higher self-esteem, get better school grades, and are less likely to become pregnant early, or have problems with alcohol or drugs. Dads are good for girls.

As this message has spread in recent years, dads are stepping up. Today's young fathers spend *three times* as long with their children each day: talking, playing, and teaching them than the fathers of a generation ago. That's a huge change.

Here are the main ways in which a father is important to a girl.

He's Strong and Safe

Very early on a small child decides whether Dad is one of two things: a source of safety and protection, or a source of danger and threat. Safety and trust are the most central feelings daughters enjoy with a good, kind dad. We need to be reminded, we grown-ups, that we are like giants to our small children, towering in the sky. I have come to think that a father should make a pledge to himself and, silently, to his small children: "I will never hit or hurt you. I will strive never ever to frighten you." Every child should be able to say, "I always feel safe with my dad."

This can be as simple as using a softer voice. Girls' hearing is more acute than that of boys. They often think you are shouting when you think you are just using a firm voice. (When our kids were small, my partner Shaaron would point out to me that my voice was far louder than I realized. I was embarrassing to take to the supermarket! But worse, I could sound scary when I thought I was just being, well, *emphatic*. This was not the kind of father that I wanted to be.)

Our physical strength has to be used for good. This strength, rather like a powerful horse or dog, has a wonderful appeal to a small girl. Dads who get down on the floor and play with their daughters, being a horse for them to ride or a monster that they can wrestle and defeat, with much struggle and noise, give them a sense of safety and also create daughters with a higher capacity for excitement. It's as if they borrow our power and make it part of them.

This early investment of fun time leads to a daughter who wants to have adventures and share activities with us all through her growing up. There is something about seeing a girl fishing with her dad, or surfing, or out walking with him on a windy Sunday afternoon, that touches the heart and bodes well for her life.

He Stays Connected

Most new dads experience a rush of amazement, responsibility, and protective care when their little girl is born. The question, though, is, "Will he stay engaged?" In the past, confused about their role, or awkward about taking it up, just too busy, or, worst of all, not interested, many twentieth-century dads failed the test. Their daughters carried this as a deep wound. Misbehavior in the teenage years, rude and rebellious acting out and, worst of all, trashing themselves with careless boys, booze, drugs, and cars was the way daughters took revenge.

Not being loved by a dad can make a girl not love herself. Moms can compensate for this, but not completely. This was the tragedy of the industrial era, when dads worked long hours and came home exhausted. Just as for the mother when a marriage breaks down, the children often blame themselves for a breakdown in their relationship with their dad; daughters conclude that "if dad is too busy to have time for me, it must be that I am boring and not worth it."

When I talk about fathers to audiences of parents, there is always a point where I see women around the auditorium quietly shedding a tear as they listen. Some are grieving for what they *didn't* get, and some are remembering the love they *did* receive. It's an intense, powerful, and life-changing relationship, a dad and his daughter.

A Practice Man

For a girl, Dad is her personal ambassador from the Planet Male. He teaches her what to expect from men. A girl can practice joking, arguing, and talking over deep things with Dad, and these skills can carry into her friendships with boys later on. She will be more confident and resistant to manipulation. If her dad treats her with respect, she won't settle for less from the males in her life.

Psychologists have found that mothers and fathers play complementary roles with daughters. Put very simply, mothers make girls *secure*, but dads give them *self-esteem*. Mom supports her daughter like a rock, steady and solid. Dad lifts her up, like a helicopter. If a girl knows that her dad is interested in her, asks her viewpoint about things (and doesn't then argue against them or knock them down), she gets the feeling that she is intelligent and worthwhile. If he takes her to the mall on a Saturday to get a glue gun, and stops off for a hot chocolate or ice cream on the way home, she can't avoid the conclusion that she is interesting for her own sake: "He likes my company!" She notices that he is not hurrying, that she is not a task he has to cross off his list. She is the destination.

Tragically Ignored

A friend of mine goes out with his teenage daughter most Saturday mornings. They sit down and have a talk, because a lot of the week he is busy and comes home late. One day they see a girl she knows from school, walking by with her dad! They greet the pair, but some instinct tells them not to invite them to join them, and anyhow, this time is sacred and they like to keep it that way. As they disappear, my friend comments, "That's nice, they are doing the same thing." His daughter isn't so sure. She explains, "Gemma's parents just got divorced. She has to spend weekends with her dad." Later, when they walk along the street they see the girl and her father sitting in a coffee shop. But they are not talking. He is holding the newspaper in front of him like a big wall. His daughter, nursing her coffee, looks like she would rather be a thousand miles away. It just looks so terribly sad.

Actions say it all. Some dads (who might consider themselves good fathers) barely *talk* to their daughters; they merely live in the same house. At least, that's how it feels to the daughter. Other dads have chosen to be a real presence. They check in with her every day, and take time to listen, or even have some regular activity, like walking the dog together, that creates the chance to talk. They enquire about her life. They listen as girls talk about their friends, their projects, what they like and don't like at school. Sometimes there is a kind of ritual: "What was the worst thing that happened today?" "What was the best?"

How Not to Fight with Your Teenage Girl

They are smart, they are fast talking, they are scary, and they live in your house. Teenage girls and dads can fly off the handle with each other—pressing all the wrong buttons—that is, unless dads know about the inside secrets.

Here, buried in this book like a special sealed section, is what you need to know.

* Your daughter loves you—you've stayed around, been kind, and kept her safe and alive for umpteen years. She would be very upset if you were to die and would miss you forever.
* But all the same, she can find you very irritating. That's because you tend to criticize and find fault, and you do it at the worst times.

In hundreds of family therapy interviews, trying to find out why a teenage girl is causing trouble, it's come down to this—dads who criticize their daughters, start fights with them, and can't accept that they have different points of view. She wants to become her own person and is acutely sensitive to you trying to control her. So when you lose it, she double loses it, and it all goes haywire. Daughters have to be treated gently.

If your daughter wrote you a letter about this, here's what she might say:

Dear Dad,

I am a teenager now. It's very hard. My emotions feel like English weather. Life is stressful, what with school and boys and not liking how I look and the mess the world is in and hating my hair.

I need to chill out quite a lot—to watch some TV when I get home from school, and be vague and dreamy and waltz around the house. If you criticize me, it's just kind of the last straw. So I will yell back at you or storm off to my room. But it's not my fault. My prefrontal cortex has melted down for a rebuild and won't be right again until about age twenty-two. So my amygdala has taken over, and all it knows is fight or flight! Scare me and you can choose which one I give you back.

You think because I can outargue you that I am smart. But I have lost the most important faculty a person can have—I can't see anyone else's point of view. Or at least not easily. It's enough to keep track of my own point of view. In fact, I will try on lots of different points of view to find out if one fits. Today I am an emo-punk-Goth-angel and plan to get piercings in my cheeks. Tomorrow I might volunteer as a nurse in Angola.

You worry about boyfriends. You worry about me navigating sex. So do I! We're not on different sides.

You worry that I won't do my schoolwork. Well, how would you feel when they tell you your whole life depends on a couple of days of exams, that it could all be over at seventeen if I have a bad night or forget my pen? It's enough to paralyze you with fear.

Please—don't criticize me. I am already criticizing myself so much it just might tip me over the edge. And I'd be so upset if I killed you. Talk gently. Ask about my life. Watch the timing, I will sometimes want to talk and sometimes not. When I am, you better have a couple of hours!! Be gentle. Be funny. Be patient. One day I will be over this, and we can be the best of friends.

Your (loving) daughter

Hearing Her Out

In talking with your daughter, allow that sometimes she will be unhappy with you. If you can ask her about what you did wrong, and she tells you, don't try to defend yourself. That's a guy move, and it doesn't work with women or girls. Instead, see if you can figure out the emotion she is telling you about. Actually ask her if she is

sad (you are going away *again*),

angry (you didn't keep your word), or

afraid (you drive too fast)

and adjust your actions accordingly. Take a guess and ask her if you have understood her correctly. And then, even though you have been a perfect and impeccably faultless father, try doing something really radical and admit *you* could change a little to accommodate her. Because (in her view) she has so little power, and you have so much, if you make changes to your behavior, or do something that she asks you to do, it makes her feel wonderful that her feelings count.

More than once in the heat of a painful argument with my daughter during her teens, I would be knocked sideways by the clarity and heartfelt honesty with which she spoke and how well she was expressing how wrong I was! I'd be caught between wanting to win the argument and being so proud of her, all at the same time.

Speak from the heart and perhaps she will, too. The biggest mistake we men make in conflict times is to use "you messages." You are such a slob. You don't help around the house. You are lazy. You are not going out in that dress! But "I messages" work better. That's because they involve being vulnerable. "I was scared and worried when you didn't get home at the time you agreed. I need to know I can trust you." This is not an attack, because it starts with "I" and not "You." It invites her to be caring, not to defend herself. Even "I am angry because the kitchen was a mess, and I had just tidied it up" is better than "You messed up the kitchen!"

Sometimes kids learn from TV and the way people talk at school that they can be rude to each other and you, and that's somehow normal and okay. (In Australia, where I live, a TV sitcom from the UK called *My Family* caused us real astonishment—it seemed to consist of really unpleasant people being horrible to each other. In real life, somebody would commit suicide in a family like that.) Putting people down erodes everyone's happiness and sense of worth. It's perfectly fine to talk it over with the whole family and get an agreement that *nobody* talks disrespectfully to anyone else—parent to child, child to parent, child to child.

It's also important to establish that work has to be shared—cooking, cleaning, laundry, gardening, and pets are everyone's responsibility and it's "fair to share." Also, make sure that your services—driving her to school, helping her in myriad ways—are gladly given but are not to be taken for granted. And they could stop if they are!

Inevitably mistakes will happen, but you will stop and sort it out, say sorry, and gradually make the household a happier place. Rudeness always wounds, and if it becomes normal and accepted, people will be bleeding all the time. Doing your share is a way of saying that love is about what you *do*, not just what you say. She's going to need to know that.

No More Princess

There is a bad mistake that some dads make, especially dads who are money rich but time poor, and that is to treat their daughter like a princess. They buy her expensive gifts and let her have money without earning it. She never has to help around the house, her laundry and meals are all done for her. This leads to an interesting result—a grown-up girl with an emotional age of two. TSO—or terminal self-obsession—is an awful fate for a girl. Tantrums, demands, screeching, breaking things are all evidence that this syndrome has taken hold. The cure is to softly but firmly begin to impose boundaries and also requirements that she pull her weight. Make sure your partner is on board, work out a plan, and get help from a family therapist if you need it to get things on track. This is important, as princesses collide with reality in painful ways if parents don't help them rejoin the human race.

Being Clearly Nonsexual

There is a dark side to daughters and dads. A very small number of dads and stepdads use their daughters for sexual gratification. This can range from sexual touching through to actual rape.

The problem is not that men can see the attractiveness of their daughter or any girl (but it's wrong to ever act on this, or encourage it in oneself by giving it room in your imagination or nurture it by accessing child porn), the problem is that some men are so psychopathically selfish that they don't draw a line on this. They blur that line or cross it completely. This is always wrong, always harmful, and, of course, a crime.

A far wider problem, which probably affects most families, is that by being aware of the problem of sexual abuse, dads back away from teenage daughters, not hugging them, not spending time with them, or getting irrationally angry with them for no other reason than that they are starting to look pretty and attractive. Their daughter gets a confusing, hurtful signal that she does not understand: "He doesn't like me, he doesn't hug me anymore, he is weird and uptight around me." A girl might just feel bad about herself. She might figure out that it's something to do with getting older and more womanly and try to turn herself back into a little girl again, to be cute and helpless instead of adult and confident in herself.

A dad who is sorted out in his own head about this, who knows how to steer his own attractedness, who is close to his wife and comfortable with his daughter growing up, can affirm her beauty and wit without making her or himself uncomfortable.

The Magic of One on One

Here is a huge clue to being a dad. While you can have fun with all your children together, to really be close, that time has to be spent one on one. So sometimes have whole weekends away with just one child. Go somewhere—camp, stay in a cabin, cook, clean, talk, sleep—and you will find you get into a deeper place with each other. Do the same or something different with each child, so they know the joy and memory of having you all to themselves.

Practical Stuff

Being a hands-on dad early makes it so much easier to stay close and develop your relationship as she gets older.

START YOUNG

Through her babyhood and toddlerhood, cuddling, swishing her around, and playing horsie games on the floor with her helps her to see you as exciting and fun. Be gentle and watch her face to see she is not alarmed.

Gently reading stories or making up stories for her when she is still a toddler, as she is getting ready to fall asleep, gives your wife a spell away from the kids and is a great bonding time.

FIND COMMON INTERESTS

Read to her or make up stories when she is small. Find books or characters that you both like. Save her a spot to garden with you. Make things in the shed, go to plays or movies together. Make traditions—"Dad and I always do this . . ." A common interest like hiking or fishing might emerge. Search for the common ground, it will create a lot of good times and great memories.

LISTEN A LOT

Girls love to talk, so dads need to learn to listen. Enquire about what she is thinking about, dreaming, and wishing for in her life. Take her seriously. Ask about what is the best thing that has happened this week. And the worst. When she shares something with you that is private, don't blab it to everyone, apart from possibly her mom. Your daughter needs to know that she can trust you.

If You Are a Single Mom

It's just possible you are a single mom reading this. You could be feeling bad that your daughter doesn't have a dad she knows or who is around very much in her life. I've talked to hundreds of single moms and daughters of single moms, and here is what they have told me helps with this problem:

1. Recruit men you can really trust to be interested in her, teach her, and spend time with her. Grandfathers and uncles will be cautious about showing an interest, especially when she is in her teens, but if you ask them, she will benefit from their teaching her to do things, talking and laughing with her, being involved in her life. (Don't leave her with grown-up men on her own, but stay nearby, and both will feel safer and more at ease.) Men often need to be asked; it engages their "practical help" gene and they do a great job.

2. You yourself are a big role model. If you are angry and disappointed with men, she may be ambivalent, either feeling the same, or flipping to the other extreme and being man crazy. It's important that you get help for any issues about being hurt by men and that you relate to men with strength and dignity, but warmth, too, so that she sees you can get along with men. If you repartner, do it slowly and cautiously, with a lot of care. But don't do it unless you yourself feel really ready. Being strongly and happily single is also a good example for her in emotional independence.

WRITE NOTES AND LETTERS

When you are traveling or even just at your workplace, send her notes or an email. Her birthday is a good opportunity to write a card to her, letting her know how you feel about her and how proud you are of her. Give lots of examples from the year that has just gone by.

BE A GREAT EXAMPLE OF MANHOOD

Be clean, smell good, and dress well around her. Don't swear. Don't tell dirty jokes. Daughters have acute senses and sensibilities, and even when they are acting rough, they don't like it in their father. The way your daughter sees you treat women makes a big difference in how she will see men later in her life. Be on your best behavior with her, her mother, and other female friends and relatives. Simple courtesy and kindness will go a long way in helping her set the bar high for the men in her own life.

What Happened to Kaycee?

Remember Kaycee? I promised to let you know how things worked out for her, so here goes. When Kaycee's parents heard her story, right there in the counselor's room, they both were in tears. It was suddenly and painfully clear that they had really not been as close to their daughter, or known her inner world, anywhere near as much as she had needed. Both mother and father began, in the weeks that followed, and with the counselor's help, to work out how to set this right. It had taken years for the problem to develop, and it would be best to go carefully and with determination to make it right.

Kaycee's mom had a small business, a group of fashion shops, that absorbed much of her time and energy and had done so since her children were small. She resolved that this had taken up too much of her time—she had two younger children as well as Kaycee and was also concerned for them. She rearranged her life, with one clear goal: that she would be home when the kids came home from school. From that basis, she would begin to build a stronger connection with them. She made no promises or fanfare about this, it just simply began to happen, but it was close to 100 percent. It changed the entire feeling of their family life.

(In telling you this story, I am aware that you might well ask, Why was it the mother who had to curtail her career? All I can say is this is what this mother decided. Life isn't always ideologically right.)

Kaycee's father was, if anything, more distraught. He wanted to break heads, phone lawyers. But he was led to understand that this was, in a way, the easy route—throw some power around. What was needed was harder than that. He acknowledged, painfully and slowly, that he had been a woeful father, at least on a personal level. He, too, began to work out ways in which he could listen, attend, and show up more in his children's lives.

This dad traveled a lot with work, and it occurred to him that an upcoming job in Cairns, in tropical north Queensland, would occur during Kaycee's midyear break and that potentially she could come with him, and perhaps go snorkeling for a few days on the reef afterward. He put this idea to Kaycee, fully expecting she would snub the idea, that the last thing she'd want to do would be hang out with an old guy like him.

So he was surprised when she said yes, and looked and sounded genuinely eager. In fact, she looked vulnerable, as if thinking, "Will it really happen? Will he cancel at the last minute?" Kaycee was taking a risk; they both were vulnerable to it being a failure, and they might not get along. That's how it is with real relationships, your heart is on the line.

The trip went well. The business part took three days so Kaycee was blissed out to lie by the pool, wander around the promenade and shops, and read books. She also had the chance to observe her father in a work setting. She saw that it was not all smooth sailing, that he was under pressure, dealing with a lot, rallying a lot of energy. She realized that this was something he did every day, so as to provide for his family. But at the same time she saw that he had talents and skills and was using them for a good end. It was a side of him she hadn't seen.

Then they traveled up to Port Douglas, the Barrier Reef, and the fun part. At least that was the plan. On the first night, something small happened, a little flare-up over tidying up, Kaycee can't really remember what it was, but suddenly they were fighting and out it all came. (Perhaps you've experienced this, a small issue suddenly provides the detonator for the main explosion—all the hurts and resentments built up over months or years come bursting out.)

Kaycee really let fly. It was very specific—the time in fourth grade when she had been the solo singer in the concert. He had promised to come and then not shown up. A time he had yelled at her mother, frightening them all. But mostly his absence, his distractedness around the house, his preference for the shelter of his newspaper than the games and interests of his children.

Dave, the father, fought a huge urge to defend himself, to give reasons, to counterattack with examples of her selfishness, her deficiencies as a daughter. He kept a tight rein on this, breathed deeply, and kept listening. In fact, he asked for more information, more details. And Kaycee kept it coming!

As she wound down, she was aware of his face, and a look of remorse mixed with a kind of pride almost in her gutsiness. This wasn't a tantrum, there was real hurt and vulnerability in what she was saying. He was genuinely ashamed of causing her so much pain. That look spoke to her more than words, and the feeling between them softened.

The next day, swimming among the turtles and multihued corals, was beautiful. They chatted with other tourists. The days flew past. Father and daughter, still tentative and careful, found themselves laughing or just spending sweet quiet time, wordlessly happy to just be.

When they got home, Kaycee's mom couldn't wait to ask her how it had been. She waited until there was a good time, peaceful and private. Later that night, she spoke to Dave about it as they lay in bed. "You know, Dave, there's something I want you to hear. I don't think Kaycee would mind. I asked Kaycee how the trip had gone. She told me those were the best six days of her life."

Postscript

There's a film you should see if you have a girl. (If she's fourteen or older, she would love it too.) It's called *Made In Dagenham*, and it kind of slipped by a year or two ago because it's not about anything violent and didn't feature Angelina Jolie. It is gripping, upbeat, funny, and very memorable.

It's about how life was for women in the 1960s, and how a small group of working women in a London factory rose up and made the world change. It's a positive, quietly shocking story that makes my eyes well up every time I watch it. There is an interesting little angle to it, that the richest, most successful woman in the movie is the most oppressed. The film shows that only women can free themselves, that the world will never give you freedom, it has to be taken. It also shows how well men can respond to this, if they have open hearts.

Your daughter needs to know she is part of a bigger story, a fight that has been fought on her behalf, long before she was born, and that she needs to keep fighting. A hundred years ago a woman couldn't even vote. She couldn't leave a violent husband. She couldn't earn the same pay for the same work. Right now in Afghanistan, one in six mothers die in childbirth. In the towns of Papua, New Guinea, a queue of beaten bleeding women stands outside every hospital every weekend. In the city you live in there are women who are sex slaves. Probably children. There is work to do.

Germaine Greer, the woman who more than any other has blown the trumpet for the movement to liberate women, said it in her recent book, *The Whole Woman*: "It's time to get angry again." It's certainly time to mobilize our love and our determination, and, for all daughters everywhere, put things right.

Author's Notes

Dear Reader,

Most people don't read this part of the book. However, I have tried to tell the story of why these sources are included, and a bit more background, so you might find it worth a skim.

The research on gender differences is vast, and they have been both understated and overstated at different times. A good introduction for parents to brain differences in girls is *It's a Girl Thing* by Michael Nagel (Cheltenham, Victoria, Australia: Hawker Brownlow Education, 2008). A timely warning on not overstating gender differences is *Delusions of Gender* by Cordelia Fine (New York: W. W. Norton, 2010). This book reminds us that although there are gender differences in predisposition, these are "soft-wired," and we can greatly influence them to ensure no disadvantage or limitations are put on either gender.

The importance of mother-child attunement (page 23) is discussed with great clarity in *Motherhood: How Should We Care for Our Children?* by Anne Manne (Crows Nest, NSW, Australia: Allen and Unwin, 2005). It is an encouraging and affecting read for anyone who wants to think more deeply about being a parent in a society that doesn't make that easy.

For more of the science on joint attention sequences (page 22), see "Social Cognition, Joint Attention, and Communicative Competence from 9 to 15 Months of Age," by M. Carpenter, K. Nagell, et al. in *Monographs of the Society for Research in Child Development* (1998), Vol. 63, No. 4, i–iii, v–vi, 1–174.

See also Martin Seligman's *Helplessness: On Depression, Development and Death* (New York: W. H. Freeman and Co., 1975, 1992). Seligman went on to found the field of positive psychology.

Leaving babies to cry themselves out is a concern to many in the infant attachment field, because it endangers the sense of trust between parent and child. There are some great books on gentler ways to help children sleep, such as *The Baby Sleep Book* by William Sears, Martha Sears, Robert Sears, and James Sears (Boston: Little, Brown, 2005), and the excellent book *Helping Baby Sleep* by Anni Gethin and Beth Macgregor (Berkeley, CA: Celestial Arts, 2009).

A great summary of father-child interaction studies is in Richard Fletcher's *The Dad Factor* (Warriewood, Australia: Finch, 2011). Fletcher heads the Family Action Center at the University of Newcastle; search online for his research articles. He has done pioneering work with indigenous dads, dads in prison, and dads with postnatal depression.

Vivian Gussin Paley writes about the importance of fantasy play in *A Child's World* (Chicago: University of Chicago Press, 2005). This acclaimed book explains how important, rich, and healing children's make-believe play really is, and how to encourage it. A textbook in many courses, you can often get it cheaply secondhand. You can find a good overview of the play research field in *ECH13 Play and Inquiry in Early Childhood,* edited by S. Degotardi (London: Pearson Education, 2013).

Gender differences in parent-child emotion narratives is explored in an article by R. Fivush, M. A. Brotman, J. P. Buckner, and S. H. Goodman, in *Sex Roles,* Vol. 42, No. 3–4, 233–53.

Mary Ainsworth's work in Uganda in the 1950s established for the first time that patterns between mother and baby are universal across all cultures. With John Bowlby, she founded attachment theory, the basis of our whole understanding of how children thrive (of course, indigenous people had known this for 300,000 years). The article on "Attachments Beyond Infancy" by Mary Ainsworth (*American Psychologist,* 1989, Vol. 44, No. 4, 709–16) is just one of hundreds she wrote.

Kim Payne's message about simplifying life for children (page 41) and restoring their rhythms of activity and rest is something the world urgently needs to hear. His book with Lisa M. Ross is called *Simplicity Parenting* (New York: Ballantine, 2010). Also a good website with many resources is www.simplicityparenting.org. The wider movement to protect, slow down, and deepen the experience of childhood is authoritatively explored by many leading voices in *Too Much Too Soon,* edited by Richard House (Gloucestershire, England: Hawthorn Press, 2011).

Here's a nice change: a wonderful DVD from New Zealand called *Untouchable Girls: Topp Twins the Movie.* It's a moving story with many performances, both comedic and musical. Available at www.topptwins.com.

The Wonder of Girls by Michael Gurian (New York: Atria, 2002) is a book that divides people greatly. It is thoughtful and deep, and the Gurians are engaged parents who give detailed help on many aspects of girlhood. But it occasionally wanders wildly into what many read as biological determinism. If you are the kind of person who has friends you love but sometimes disagree with, you will be able to take the good and leave what you don't like.

Best Friends, Worst Enemies: Understanding the Social Lives of Children by Michael Thompson, Catherine O'Neill-Grace, and Lawrence J. Cohen (New York: Ballantine, 2001) is almost up there with Penelope Leach in its closeup knowledge of the world of children. One big benefit of the book can be summed up in this quote: "In my experience what interferes most strongly with a parents' wisdom in this area are the painful memories from his or her own childhood." Very helpful in *not overreacting*.

Read D. David and R. K. Lyons's article "Differential Attachment Responses of Male and Female Infants to Frightening Maternal Behavior: Tend and Befriend vs. Fight or Flight?" in *Infant Mental Health Journal* (2005), Vol. 21, No. 1, 1–18) if you are really into this stuff.

A treasure trove of good science applied to parenthood can be found at www.parentingscience.com/strange-situation.html.

Okay, fasten your seatbelt. The concerns about hormone disruptors (page 97) in everyday items like plastics, air fresheners, and supermarket receipts are so great, I have included far more documentation. First, for proof that it's happening, see S. Euling et al., "Examination of US Puberty-Timing Data from 1940 to 1994 in Secular Trends: Panel Findings." *Pediatrics* (February 1, 2008) Vol. 121 S3, S172–91. See also "Public Health Implications of Altered Puberty Timing," by M. S. Golub, G. W. Collman, P. Foster, et al. in *Pediatrics* (February 1, 2008) Vol. 121, No. S3, S218–30.

Second, for proof that it's a problem: "Children with early puberty are at a risk for accelerated skeletal maturation and short adult height, early sexual debut, potential sexual abuse, and psychosocial difficulties. Altered puberty timing is also of concern for the development of reproductive tract cancers later in life. For example, an early age of menarche is a risk factor for breast cancer. Altered timing of puberty also has implications for behavioral disorders. For example, an early maturation is associated with a greater incidence of conduct and behavior disorders during adolescence. Finally, altered puberty timing is considered an adverse effect in reproductive toxicity risk assessment for chemicals. Recent US legislation has mandated improved chemical testing approaches for protecting children's health and screening for endocrine-disrupting agents" (ibid.).

Third, for proof that BPA and pthalates have a powerful effect on babies and children, especially when exposure happens in pregnancy, see "Impact of Early-Life Bisphenol A Exposure on Behavior and Executive

Function in Children," by Joe M. Braun, et al., in *Pediatrics Online* (October 24, 2011), Vol. 128, No. 5, 873–82. "In utero exposure to the organic compound bisphenol A (BPA), widely used in the manufacture of plastics, including cups and food containers, was associated with *behavior disruptions at age 3*, particularly among girls." Increased gestational exposure to BPA also was associated with *higher depression* scores in girls. For each tenfold increase in gestational urinary BPA concentration, there was an adjusted increase in *anxiety scores*. The increase was pronounced among girls but minimal among boys, the researchers reported.

Braun and colleagues had previously found that gestational exposure was associated with hyperactivity and aggressive behavior in girls age two. But it's not only children who are affected. "A 2008 study published in the *Journal of American Medicine* looked at urinary BPA levels in 1,455 US adults. The result: The higher the BPA concentration in people's urine, the higher their incidence of cardiovascular trouble and diabetes," according to I. A. Lang, T. S. Galloway, et al., in an article entitled "Association of Urinary Bisphenol A Concentration with Medical Disorders and Laboratory Abnormalities in Adults, published in the *Journal of the American Medical Association* (September 2008), Vol. 300, No. 11, 1303–10.

What to do about it?

Previous research has suggested that avoiding food packaged in plastic may lessen the impact, advice that was echoed by Braun and colleagues. Canned soup was identified as a particular concern. "The FDA's own research shows that BPA leaches from can linings into food, and a 2011 Harvard study found BPA at heightened levels in people who regularly consume canned soup."

And it doesn't take much, according to Jenny Carwile, Henry Luu, et al., who wrote "Polycarbonate Bottle Use and Urinary Bisphenol A Concentrations," in *Environmental Health Perspectives* (September, 2009), Vol. 117. "A Harvard study supports what many public health specialists have long assumed: Hard plastic drinking bottles containing bisphenol A are leaching notable amounts of the controversial chemical into people's bodies."

And here's some more just in case you're in any doubt:

Ian Austen. "Canada Takes Steps to Ban Most Plastic Baby Bottles," *New York Times,* April 19, 2008.

D. Caserta, L. Maranghi, and A. Mantovani, "Impact of Endocrine Disruptor Chemicals in Gynaecology," *Human Reproduction Update* (2008), Vol. 14, No. 1, 59–72.

I. Colon, D. Caro, C. J. Bourdony, and O. Rosario, "Identification of Phthalate Esters in the Serum of Young Puerto Rican Girls with Premature Breast Development, *Environ Health Perspective* (2000), Vol. 108, 895–900.

B. S. Reddy, R. Rozati, B. V. Reddy, and N. V. Raman, "Association of Phthalate Esters with Endometriosis in Indian Women, *BJOG* (May, 2006), Vol. 113, No. 5, 515–20.

S. Sathyanarayana, "Phthalates and Children's Health," *Current Problems Pediatric Adolescent Health Care* (February, 2008), Vol. 38, 34–49.

L. N. Vandenberg, R. Hauser, M. Marcus, et al. "Human Exposure to Bisphenol A (BPA)." *Reproductive Toxicology* (2007), Vol. 24, 139–77.

To hear Peter Benson's inspiring and moving talk about spark (page 80), go to YouTube and search under Benson and spark. The video is actually a TED talk. Peter's book *Sparks: How Parents Can Ignite the Hidden Strengths of Teenagers* (Hoboken, NJ: Jossey-Bass, 2008) includes quizzes, questionnaires, and other research-based materials to help you and your child find her spark and follow it through. Or you can visit the website www.search-institute.org/sparks.

The poem by Pamela Du-Valle about coming out (page 103) appears in *When Our Children Come Out* by Maria Pallotta-Chiarolli (Sydney, Australia: Finch, 2005). More of Pamela's poems are at www.angelfire.com/pq/pam/poems.html.

You can find out more about Pathways to Womanhood (page 108) and Pathways to Manhood at www.pathwaysfoundation.com.au. Pathways is community based and works with parents in their own area to create the event for their girls.

The information about Missy Higgins (page 115) draws from a feature article entitled "Out of the Dark" by journalist Chris Johnston. It appeared in *Good Weekend* magazine, May 19, 2012. A similar article with additional information appeared in the *Sunday Tasmanian*. See also "Missy Higgins' Secret Musical Crisis" by C. Adams in the *Herald Sun*, April 4, 2012.

A fuller description of how to use "stand and think" (page 50) safely and kindly with children can by found in *The Complete Secrets of Happy Children*, and also in *More Secrets of Happy Children* by Steve and Shaaron Biddulph (London: Thorsons, 2006).

More about adolescent sleep patterns (page 117) can be found in the following:

M. A. Carskadon (Ed.), *Adolescent Sleep Patterns: Biological, Social, and Psychological Influences* (Cambridge, England: Cambridge University Press, 2002).

J. Owens, K. Belon, and P. Moss, "Impact of Delaying School Start Time on Adolescent Sleep, Mood, and Behavior," *Archives of Pediatric and Adolescent Medicine* (2010) Vol. 164, No. 7, 608–14.

Amy R. Wolfson and Mary A. Carskadon, "Understanding Adolescents' Sleep Patterns and School Performance: A Critical Appraisal," *Sleep Medicine Review* (2003), Vol. 7, No. 6, 491–506.

Amy R. Wolfson and Mary A. Carskadon, "Sleep Schedules and Daytime Functioning in Adolescents," *Child Development* (1998), Vol. 69, 875–87.

A good overview of the mental health crisis affecting young people is R. Eckersley's "Troubled Youth: An Island of Misery in a Sea of Happiness, Or the Tip of an Iceberg of Suffering?" *Intervention in Psychiatry* (2011), Vol. 5, Suppl. 1, 6–11. Stephen Hinshaw's *The Triple Bind: Saving Our Teenage Girls from Today's Pressures* (New York: Ballantine, 2009) gives stunning incidence figures for rising suicide, violence, mental health admissions, self-harm, and alcohol and eating-disorder problems for girls worldwide. Hinshaw is a professor of psychology at the University of California at Berkeley.

Alcohol manufacturers, retailers, and shareholders profit from causing untold harm to our young, according to researchers and public health campaigners. An article by Dr. Ramesh Manocha (www.generation next.com.au/2012/08/how-alcohol-ads-target-kids) sums up the advertising impacts on teen drinking:

"Parents might do their best to shield their kids from advertising related to alcohol, but alcohol marketers are doing their best to reach them anyway. That's the finding of new research that discovered that the content of alcohol ads placed in magazines is more likely to violate industry guidelines if the ad appears in a magazine with sizable youth readership.

"The research, which was done by the Center on Alcohol Marketing and Youth (CAMY) at the Johns Hopkins Bloomberg School of Public Health, found that ads in magazines with a substantial youth readership (15 percent or more) frequently showed alcohol being consumed in an irresponsible manner. Examples include showing alcohol consumption near or on bodies of water, encouraging overconsumption, and providing messages supportive of alcohol addiction. In addition, nearly one in five ad occurrences contained sexual connotations or sexual objectification.

"As at least 14 studies have found that the more young people are exposed to alcohol advertising and marketing, the more likely they are to drink, or if

already drinking, to drink more, this report should serve as a wake-up call to parents and everyone else concerned about the health of young people.

The researchers examined 1,261 ads for alco-pops, beer, spirits or wine that appeared more than 2,500 times in 11 different magazines that have or are likely to have disproportionately youthful readerships. Ads were analyzed for different risk codes: injury content, overconsumption content, addiction content, sex-related content and violation of industry guidelines. This latter category refers to the voluntary codes of good marketing practice administered by alcohol industry trade associations.

According to CAMY, alcohol is responsible for 4,700 deaths per year among young people under the age of 21, and is associated with the three leading causes of death among youth: motor vehicle crashes, homicide and suicide."

The marketing of alcohol to the young should be made illegal.

For more about sexual behavior of adolescents, check out "Sexual Behavior and Related Knowledge Among a Representative Sample of High School Students Between 1997 and 2008" by P. A. Agius, M. K. Pitts, et al. in *Australian Research Center in Sex, Health and Society, Australian and New Zealand Journal of Public Health* (2010), Vol. 34, No. 5, 476–81. The authors write:

" [T]he marked increase in students, particularly those in senior year, having sexual intercourse with multiple partners is also significant. Factors such as early age of sexual debut and relationship formation, and increased alcohol consumption have been associated with increases in the number of sexual partnerships of adolescents . . . and these may also be symptomatic of a more broader cultural change in adolescent sexuality and identity. In Australia, rates of alcohol consumption among secondary students have increased markedly, as has the proportion of young people engaging in sex while under the influence of alcohol or drugs . . ."

The best and most moving descriptions of how community and adult connectedness has disappeared for our girls come from the books of Mary Pipher. Highly recommended is *Reviving Ophelia: Saving the Selves of Adolescent Girls* (New York: Penguin, 2002) and *The Shelter of Each Other* (New York: Penguin, 2008).

Set Free Childhood by Martin Large (Melbourne, Australia: Hawthorn Press, 2003) provides an excellent summary of the research into children and media. It deals especially well with the brain and the developmental harms of too many screens and the overly passive use of playing time. It's a popular book aimed at parents. For more on the subject, check out:

"Media Guidelines for Parents," *American Academy of Pediatrics* (n.d.). Retrieved August 24, 2006, from www.aap.org. The American Academy of Pediatrics recommends no more than one to two hours of quality TV and videos a day for older children and no screen time for children under the age of two. They also specify that parents should keep TV sets, VCRs, video games, and computers out of children's bedrooms.

Dilemmas of Desire: Teenage Girls Talk About Sexuality by Deborah L. Tolman (Boston: Harvard University Press, 2005) is an excellent book for parents wanting to be life-affirming rather than negative in their approach to their daughter's sexuality.

Australia's National Centre Against Bullying is a superb resource for schools, parents, and children. Visit their website at www.ncab.org.au.

Some statistics:

One student in every four in Australian schools is affected by bullying.

Kids who are bullied are three times more likely to show depressive symptoms, says the Center for Adolescent Health.

Children who were bullied were up to nine times more likely to have suicidal thoughts, say some studies.

Girls who were victims of bullying in their early elementary school years were more likely to remain victims as they got older, according to British research.

Children who were frequently bullied by their peers were more likely to develop psychotic symptoms in their early adolescence, says more UK research.

Girls were much more likely than boys to be victims of both cyber and traditional bullying, says a recent Murdoch Children's Research Institute study.

Children as young as three can become victims of bullying, says Canadian research.

Young people who bully have a one in four chance of having a criminal record by the age of thirty.

Bullying is the fourth most common reason young people seek help from children's help services.

A good guide to changing the culture and climate in schools to reduce bullying is found in *Friendly Schools Plus Evidence for Practice*. STEPS Professional Development (ISBN 978 1 021321) by D. Cross, S. Thompson, S. Waters, N. Pearce, L. Thomas, L., 2012.

Also look at Rosalind Wiseman's book (discussed on page 136) *Queen Bees and Wannabes: Helping Your Daughter Survive Cliques, Gossip, Boyfriends, and the New Realities of Girl World* (New York: Three Rivers Press, 2009). Rosalind also has an excellent website with a great deal of video content: www.rosalindwiseman.com.

Maggie Hamilton's book (discussed on page 4) is *What's Happening to Our Girls?* (New York: Viking/Penguin, 2009). A wonderful book for girls, a practical networking and ideas book about being creative, with beautiful inspiring ideas for making and doing interspersed with wise help is Hamilton's *Secret Girls' Business* (New York: Penguin, 2012).

A final work on bullying, "Empathy Tactic Fails on Worst Bullies" by N. Brady in *The Age*, August 19, 2012, reports on research to be released by Kate Hadwen's team in late 2012.

There are numerous resources for eating disorders:

The National Eating Disorders Association website can be found at www.nationaleatingdisorders.org.

Linda Bacon, *Health at Every Size: The Surprising Truth about Your Weight* (San Francisco: BenBella Books: 2010).

Linda Bacon and L. Aphramor, "Weight Science: Evaluating the Evidence for a Paradigm Shift," *Nutrition Journal Online* (2011), 10:69, doi:10.1186/1475-2891-10-9.

A. Field, S. Austin, C. Taylor, et al., "Relation Between Dieting and Weight Change among Preadolescents and Adolescents," *Pediatrics* (2003), Vol. 112, No. 4, 900–6.

S. Grabe, M. Ward, and J. Hyde, "The Role of the Media in Body Image Concerns among Women: A Meta-analysis of Experimental and Correlational Studies," *Psychological Bulletin* (2008), Vol. 134, No. 3, 460–76.

J. Lumeng, P. Forrest, D. Appugliese, et al., "Weight Status as a Predictor of Being Bullied in Third through Sixth Grades," *Pediatrics* (2010), Vol. 125, No. 6, 1301–7.

D. Neumark-Sztainer, M. Wall, J. Guo, et al., "Obesity, Disordered Eating, and Eating Disorders in a Longitudinal Study of Adolescents: How Do Dieters Fare 5 Years Later?" *Journal of the American Dietetic Association* (2006), Vol. 106, 559–68.

S. Priya, L. Prendergast, E. Delbridge, K. Purcell, et al., "Long-term Persistence of Hormonal Adaptations to Weight Loss," *New England Journal of Medicine* (2011), Vol. 365, 1597–1604.

J. O'Dea, Prevention of Child Obesity: "First, Do No Harm," *Health Education Research* (2005), Vol. 20, No. 2, 259–65.

J. Treasure, K. Tchanturia, and U. Schmidt, "Developing a Model of the Treatment for Eating Disorders: Using Neuroscience Research to Examine the How Rather Than the What of Change, *Counseling and Psychotherapy Research* (2005), Vol. 5, No. 3, 1–12.

Lydia Turner, "Look Good by Doing Very Little," Australian Broadcasting Corporation, *The Drum*, July 9, 2010. Retrieved from www.abc.net.au/unleashed/36460.html.

National Eating Disorders Association, "The Impact of Media Images on Body Image and Behavior: A Summary of the Scientific Evidence" (press release). Retrieved August 2, 2012 from www.nationaleatingdisorders.org

I'm grateful to Paul Dillon for his help in writing the chapter on alcohol and other drugs (chapter 10) and providing the statistics and examples. Paul's website is www.darta.net.au. Paul's book, *Teenagers, Alcohol and Drugs* (Sydney, Australia: Allen and Unwin, 2009) is an excellent and eye-opening book about what are the real concerns, and what are not. It's a positive, easy to read, and has many stories. We need to know about what our kids encounter if we are to help them.

Check out S. Lewis, N. Heath, et al., "Helpful or Harmful? An Examination of Viewers Responses to Nonsuicidal Self-Injury Videos on YouTube," *Journal of Adolescent Health Online*, October 2012.

For more on stepmothers (page 176), see "A Portrait of Stepfamilies," Pew Research Center Report (January 13, 2011), accessed from www.pewsocialtrends.org/2011/01/13/a-portrait-of-stepfamilies.

See N. Gibbs's article "The Magic of the Family Meal," *Time Magazine*, June 4, 2006. Kids who eat with their parent/s each night have stunningly better outcomes (though its possible the family meal is an expression of a family being calm, ordered, and friendly as much as a cause). Eating together produces oxytocin, the hormone that makes people like each other. The research also found its the *regularity* of having family meals that does the trick (at least, for the evening meal of the day). Try it for a month, and see for yourself.

For more on girls and their parents, see Steve Bidduph, *The New Manhood* (Sydney, Australia: Finch, 2010) and Germaine Greer, *The Whole Woman* (New York: Anchor, 2000).

Contributors and Acknowledgments

Paula Joye is a journalist and fashion writer. She was formally the editor of *Cleo* and *Madison* magazines, and she is currently editor of www.lifestyled.com.au and the Fashion and Style columnist for Fairfax Media.

Kym Pitman is an Australian singer-songwriter whose albums include the acclaimed *Million Star Hotel*. Kym founded the Bellingen Wilderness Youth Theatre, a unique rite of passage for young people integrating wilderness treks with theatre and music. Kim writes and teaches about the value of wilderness in young people's development into healthy adulthood www.kympitman.com.

Dr. Michael Carr-Gregg is Australia's best-known psychologist and authority on adolescent mental health. He founded the national organization for teenage cancer patients, CanTeen, is an associate professor at the University of Melbourne's Department of Paediatrics, and created the National Centre Against Bullying (www.ncab.org.au). Michael is the author of *Surviving Adolescents* (2005), *The Princess Bitchface Syndrome* (2006), *Real Wired Child* (2007), *Surviving Step Families* (2011), *Surviving Year 12* (2012), and *When to Really Worry* (2010).

Lydia Jade Turner is a psychotherapist specializing in eating disorders and unhealthy weight loss behaviors. In addition she works with those affected by bariatric surgery, "obesity," sexual assault, trauma, and gender-related difficulties. A staunch critic of the diet industry, Lydia regularly presents at conferences worldwide. She is the manager of advocacy, education, and social health at BodyMatters Clinic (www.bodymatters.com.au).

Sarah McMahon is a psychologist who specializes in the treatment of eating disorders. She is the manager of clinical and consultancy services at BodyMatters Clinic in Sydney Australia. Sarah has over a decade's experience in counseling people affected by disordered eating behaviors, facilitating eating disorder support groups and educating the community about eating pathology, in corporations, public hospitals, nongovernmental organizations and private practice (www.bodymatters.com.au).

Paul Dillon is Australia's foremost drug and alcohol educator. His best-selling book *Teenagers, Alcohol and Drugs* was released in 2009. Paul wrote the instruction manual for the NSW Police Services on alcohol and violence, and developed the United Nations UNODC Global Youth Training Workshop on amphetamine use among young people. For information on Paul's work go to www.darta.net.au.

Melinda Tankard Reist is an Australian feminist, media commentator, and advocate for women and girls. Melinda is author of *Giving Sorrow Words* (2000), *Defiant Birth: Women Who Resist Medical Eugenics* (2006), *Getting Real: Challenging the Sexualization of Girls* (2009), and co-editor with Abigail Bray of *Big Porn Inc: Exposing the Harms of the Global Pornographic Industry* (2011), all published by Spinifex Press (www.melindatankardreist.com).

Maggie Hamilton is a New Zealand–based writer, social researcher and publisher who has campaigned widely about the deteriorating mental health of girls. Her books include *What's Happening to Our Girls?* (2009) and *What's Happening to Our Boys?* (2011). Her most recent book aimed at girls is *Secret Girls Business* (2012), a beautifully crafted guide to creativity and individuality as an antidote to conformity and competition (www.maggiehamilton.org).

Collective Shout is a network of women professionals who campaign against the sexual exploitation of girls. Their friendship and inspiration made this book a far better one. You can subscribe or get involved at http://collectiveshout.org

Micky Foss is a psychotherapist and mother in Lismore, Australia. She specializes in gestalt, family, and couples therapy.

Dr. Bruce Robinson is the author of *Daughters and their Dads* (2013), and *Fathering From the Fast Lane* (2001). He is a thoracic physician, a professor of medicine, and the author of over 150 published papers. Bruce founded the Fathering Project at the University of Western Australia, and speaks about fatherhood around the globe. The Project's very moving DVD "What Kids Really Need From Their Dads" greatly influenced me as a dad, and is a great resource for encouraging fathers (www.thefatheringproject.org).

I also wish to thank Rex Finch and Samantha Miles for their careful work on this book. Sean Doyle at Lynk Manuscript Services for patient and wise help.

Carole Tonkinson, Simon Gerratt and Kathy Dyke in London. Mauro Halfeld and Luciane Clausen in Brazil and all the translators, editors, and those involved in typesetting and printing the book worldwide. I hope you are proud of it.

Especial thanks to Alison Howard, Jane Geeson, and Louise Mitchell for their detailed, invaluable help and feedback with the manuscript. They made a huge difference.

Julie Gale at Kids Free 2B Kids. To Johanna. To Linda Dalton, and Arne Rubenstein. To Caroline Richards. To Kate Hadwen. To Esther Kennedy, Lauris Pandolfini, Jane Bezzina, and Ramesh Manocha for all those amazing seminars. Ariana Biddulph for research assistance, a scientific mindset, and teaching me to laugh in adverse circumstances! And Kirsty McGeoch for first telling me about Peter Brenson and the idea of spark.

To Kim John Payne. To Doro Marden. To Shaaron, for showing me how.

And to Kaycee, Marielle, Genevieve, and their families. Well done.

Steve Biddulph's website is www.stevebiddulph.com

Index